Out of OBLIVION

Out of
OBLIVION

Awareness of the Abiding Presence
of God in Your Everyday

CATHY NORTEY

Out of OBLIVION

COPYRIGHT © 2023 Cathy Nortey

Additional copyright is on page 133.

In this publication, the author has capitalised pronouns that refer to God the Father, the Son, and the Holy Spirit. This differs from the typical publishing style.

Hardback ISBN: **978-1-7395737-2-0**
Paperback ISBN: **978-1-7395737-1-3**

Layout Design: AB Innovations *andydrewben@gmail.com*

For any correspondence with the author, please visit:
www.sevenflamingtorches.com

To my dear husband, Ebenezer, you always believed in me and encouraged me to bring this book to life, even before I had the words to articulate my thoughts.

To my three extraordinary children, Janice, Kayla, and Jedidiah, thank you for allowing me the space to create and the support I needed to make my book a reality. I love you all more than words can express.

To my parents, Harry and Sophia, you have carried the flame of God with such genuineness and love that I am privileged to be a product of such heavenly bliss. Thank you for inspiring me to keep seeking and dwelling in His presence.

To my dearest friend, Laura, you have cheered me on in the full and the empty; I am eternally grateful for that.

Contents

ACKNOWLEDGEMENTS

My Lord, my God, my Father, my Friend, my Anchor, and my Papa. You knew me, You know me, and You will always know me, and that is enough.

I am deeply grateful for the quick responses from frienditors, Faith, Laura and Mosunmola who willingly offered to proofread my project.

My Gatekeepers family, you have been our rock, giving us purpose to fulfil God's assignments. Thank you for being an integral part of my journey.

A heartfelt gratitude to Selorm for her editorial input and to Andy for his creativity. Your contributions have made a significant difference, and I am grateful.

Thank you, GCSSM family, for transforming my life with your joy and equipping me with the truths about my identity in the finished works of the Cross. Getting to know you over the past year has been an absolute delight.

I want to thank my beloved Reading Family Church for providing my family and me with an amazing church home. I am grateful for the many opportunities given to me to grow under the grace of God.

PREFACE

Oblivion - /ə'blɪv·i·ən/ - *the state of being unconscious or lacking awareness of what is happening around you.*

I lived in the dark for a long time, unaware of everything available to me. At last, I was yanked out of that state. My journey of learning about my Papa is ongoing as I strive to gain knowledge every day.

"Yet all of the accomplishments that I once took credit for, I've now forsaken them and I regard it all as nothing compared to the delight of experiencing Jesus Christ as my Lord! To truly know him meant letting go of everything from my past and throwing all my boasting on the garbage heap. It's all like a pile of manure to me now, so that I may be enriched in the reality of knowing Jesus Christ and embrace him as Lord in all of his greatness. My passion is to be consumed with him and not cling to my own "righteousness" based in keeping the written Law. My only "righteousness" will be his, based on the faithfulness of Jesus Christ—the very righteousness that comes from God."

Philippians 3:7-9, TPT

INTRODUCTION

*A*re you struggling to find meaningful time to connect with God? Is your life so crowded with activities that you cannot hear what God is clearly saying to you? Are you tired of church friends testifying about their heavenly encounters while you struggle to read a single Bible verse? Do you desperately long for authentic connections with people who genuinely care about you? Does everything around you spin so fast that you are constantly playing catch-up? If so, know that you are not alone!

For a long time, I grappled with these feelings. As a newlywed, deeply in love and surrounded by all that life had to offer, I also felt a deep, dark void in my heart. I felt lost, lonely and empty, searching for something I could not define. This life of OBLIVION led me on a convoluted journey over several years, and during that time, I learned how to abide in God's presence.

Despite the abundance of resources available, you might still realise there is a constant battle with the dissatisfied feeling of *"a lack of somethingness"* within yourself. Amid your busy lifestyle, you may struggle to connect and find acceptance and validation.

We are all born with a deep desire to be loved, accepted, and valued. The secret many people never discover is that this intimacy that our soul craves and desires can only be filled by one source: **Jesus Christ.**

He is the image of the invisible God, the firstborn of all creation: for by Him all things were created, both in the heavens and on earth, visible and invisible, whether thrones, or dominions, or rulers, or authorities—all things have been created through Him and for Him. He is before all things, and in Him all things hold together. He is also the head of the body, the church; and He is the beginning, the firstborn from the dead, so that He Himself will come to have first place in everything. For it was the Father's good pleasure for all the fullness to dwell in Him, and through Him to reconcile all things to Himself, whether things on earth or things in heaven, having made peace through the blood of His cross.

Colossians 1:15-20, NASB

Recently, I sat in a group meeting with a bunch of women and men gathered for one main purpose: to hear from and connect with God. The encounter left everyone feeling supernaturally connected and inspired, equipped with the tools to seek God's presence each day. Personally, it was a rejuvenating experience for me. I came away more aware of God's presence and His desire to connect with me.

This experience made me realise how many others need such moments and opportunities to connect with God intimately.

I was once in OBLIVION, unaware that the entire time I felt lost, I was actually lost in Him, and He was right there with me. This book is an opportunity to read about my journey as I learned to live in the daily awareness of God's presence. I hope this book's contents will offer you truths and tools to navigate your everyday life in God's abiding presence. God is with you every day and in every moment. He is close to you and desires you to be aware of His presence wherever you are.

I have outlined key strategies for incorporating God into your daily life. Whether you go from bed to school gate to boardroom or from bed to home office, whether you are in trouble, facing trauma, or even in prison, you can discover ways to connect with God amidst the chaos of life.

Are you ready to step out of OBLIVION? Because on the other side of where you are, light is beaming through, and truth is resounding. That truth declares: **God is with you right where you are**, and this book will awaken your senses to His presence with you. It will fill your spirit and soul with fresh expectations and excitement for all God has planned for you.

You will finally be able to respond to the numerous ways the Creator of the universe interacts with His creation. No matter what sphere of life you find yourself in, God wants to make Himself present, especially in your mundane and routine activities when it seems like He cannot be there. In those very moments, you will find Him right by your side and within you. He is constantly speaking to you and sharing His thoughts. He is aware of the thoughts in your head and knows the words in your mouth before you even say them. Like the Psalmist, you will become convinced of just how close He is to you:

> *Lord, you know everything there is to know about me. You perceive every movement of my heart and soul, and you understand my every thought before it even enters my mind. You are so intimately aware of me, Lord. You read my heart like an open book and you know all the words I'm about to speak before I even start a sentence! You know every step I will take before my journey even begins.*
>
> **Psalm 139:1-4, TPT**

Join me on this journey as we say *adieu* to a life of OBLIVION, where there is no awareness or consciousness of God's presence in your day-to-day life, and say hello to God's omnipresence. You are a winner inside and out. Despite what life's realities may suggest, a wonderful life awaits you and your Father will guide you there.

By the time you finish reading this book, you will savour God's abiding presence in your everyday from the moment you wake up.

What to expect from this book:

➢ **Diverse Bible translations**: Throughout my journey, I have been exposed to various Bible translations that each offer unique perspectives on God's Big Story. As a result, this book incorporates a range of translations that have influenced and shaped the narrative.

➢ **Reflection questions:** At the end of each chapter, you will find thought-provoking questions that encourage personal reflection and application.

➢ **Activations:** Discover exercises designed to deepen your intimacy with God.

➢ **Practical guides:** In addition to the main content, you will find helpful guides on various topics covered in the book, providing further guidance and application.

As you embark on this journey through the pages, I encourage you to have a pen and notebook handy. Be prepared for the unexpected ways God will show up throughout your reading experience.

There are a few options for how to engage with this book. You can read it alone, allowing yourself to fully absorb and experience the impact of God's presence. Alternatively, you may opt for a group study, reading and discussing one chapter at a time. This book can also be used as a daily devotional for personal or family time.

I hope you thoroughly enjoy reading and exploring the content of this book!

One

The Invitation

The Lord is my shepherd.
I have everything I need.
Psalm 23:1, ICB

I t all began as a casual friendship. Despite sitting in the same class together for a couple of years, he was the one person who wasn't drawn to me. I attended a secondary school for girls, which was, in my opinion, the best in Ghana. Okay, as I said, I went to a school with a reputation for turning out women who people found a little intimidating, and initially, he was suitably intimidated.

We never spoke to each other for the first two years of our undergraduate studies. I found him fascinating, but he was not the sort of person I wanted to engage with in my class. He had a knack for making a dramatic entrance and distracting the class if the lecturer allowed it. That type of person did not fit into my circle of friends. We had nothing in common and followed our separate paths during those first two years. Then, one day, out of the blue, I turned up at his accommodation, and a very dear friend introduced Ebenezer and me properly.

Before I knew it, I was smitten by love, much to everyone's astonishment. Well, there were two categories of reactions. While his friends were annoyed because I had *"taken"* their friend from them, the members of my church were disappointed because I was the pastor's daughter, and he was not a pastor's son. So, it's fair to say we had minimal support from the start.

To our surprise, we endured the ups and downs of our relationship, not only through university but also beyond graduation. Though intriguing, the tale of how we managed to do this is a story for another occasion. It was widely believed that most university relationships fizzled out after graduation, as they were not ready for the challenges of the real world. Yet, our story defied this belief.

Even when Ebenezer decided to travel to the United Kingdom (UK) right after graduation, we kept it going. The same force that held us together in the initial stages continued to keep us together despite our (mostly my) best efforts to break us up. So, through whatever means, we lasted for a long time and then he sent me an invitation!

He started something completely new while he was in the UK and wanted me to be there for him at his graduation. I received this invitation with nervousness, excitement and a wide range of see-sawing emotions. Finally, I will be reunited with my man after all this time!

I prepared all the necessary documents for my visa application and my parents spared no effort in securing the financial support required to ensure I received a positive response to my visa application.

For the first time, I entered the UK embassy. As intimidating and rigorous as the process was, I was determined and hopeful that this was IT for me. It was not my first time in an embassy; I had already travelled abroad a few months prior, so I was familiar with the visa process and had certain expectations. When I arrived at the UK embassy, I expected the royal treatment.

Despite the visa application horror stories I had heard from many people, I was wildly convinced my case would be different. I navigated several queues, followed instructions, underwent interviews, and filled out more forms. Getting a stamp on my passport was a long and stressful process.

The primary connection and justification stated on the application was that I was going to visit my fiancé. We were praying that fiancé, being a stronger connection than boyfriend but weaker than husband, would be enough justification to enable me to join him in the UK for his graduation. I convinced myself this would be enough.

I returned home fully confident and assured that all the effort would pay off and I would be with my fiancé in a few days. It was time to start packing and saying my goodbyes because I was off to join Ebenezer for his graduation ceremony.

All that glitters is not gold; I didn't get my fairytale ending. I got a letter that my visa application was unsuccessful. I was demoralised and heartbroken. Apparently, the fiancé was not a strong enough connection, after all.

We overcame our disappointment, continued our long-distance relationship and eventually married. He returned to Ghana a few months after the wedding, ready for me to join him in the UK to spend the rest of our lives together.

For the second time, I found myself at the UK embassy. I had to face my nemesis and go through the visa application process again. The difference was that this time around, Ebenezer was not my fiancé but my husband; we had a concrete union between us and a marriage certificate as evidence.

Our story reminded me of the relationship we have with God. Through His Son, Jesus Christ, God has extended an invitation to us. We have direct access to the Father because of Christ's sacrifice on the cross. God has reached out His hand to invite us into His story.

> *And now, because we are united to Christ, we both have equal and direct access to the realm of the Holy Spirit to come before the Father!*
>
> **Ephesians 2:18, TPT**

Just as I received the invitation because I became Ebenezer's wife, you also received this invitation because you are Jesus' bride. The Son sacrificed Himself for you, granting you free access to the Father and the resources of heaven through the blood of Jesus. Your Heavenly Father has pulled you in and invited you to be part of His story.

> *And now we are brothers and sisters in God's family because of the blood of Jesus, and he welcomes us to come into the most holy sanctuary in the heavenly realm—boldly and without hesitation. For he has dedicated a new, life-giving way for us to approach God. For just as the veil was torn in two, Jesus' body was torn open to give us free and fresh access to him! And since we now have a magnificent High Priest to welcome us into God's house, we come closer to God and approach him with an open heart, fully convinced that nothing will keep us at a distance from him. For our hearts have been sprinkled with blood to remove impurity, and we have been freed from an accusing conscience. Now we are clean, unstained, and presentable to God inside and out!*
>
> **Hebrews 10:19-22, TPT**

In Genesis 3, when Adam and Eve were sent out of the Garden of Eden, they were separated from God's presence. They lost access to all the resources God had freely and generously given them. God placed angels at the garden entrance to prevent their return, leaving humanity struggling to connect with God.

For many years, the children of Israel endured forced slavery in Egypt, but God had set a plan in motion to liberate and draw His children back into fellowship with Him. This plan involved various sacrifices, one of the most profound being the *"Passover"*. During this event, the Israelites marked their doorframes with the blood of a lamb to protect their firstborns from the angel of death.

A tragic event unfolded in every Egyptian home without the lamb's blood seal—the death of the firstborns. The wailings and sadness that filled the air that night were heart-wrenching. The Egyptians awoke to unimaginable grief because they lacked the insight to save themselves with the lamb's blood, as recounted in Exodus 12.

However, in the Israelite camp, there was celebration. No death occurred because of the protective mark from the lamb's blood. This act of faith saved all the Israelites that day. If any Israelites had disregarded Moses' instructions and failed to mark their doorposts, they would have experienced death and mourning within their households.

Due to the tragedy Pharaoh and his people experienced because of this sacrifice and the divine intervention it symbolised, Pharaoh finally relented and granted the Israelites their freedom to leave Egypt.

Following their exodus from Egypt, Moses gave the Israelites numerous instructions to guide them in righteous living. Books like Deuteronomy and Leviticus contain these laws, demonstrating God's persistent efforts to draw humanity closer to Him.

However, the Israelites struggled to live holy lives despite God's assistance. Eventually, at the appointed time, God sent His only Son to pay the ultimate price for humanity's salvation. John says in chapter one that Jesus came into the world He created, but His own people did not accept Him. Religious leaders particularly rejected Him, and He experienced the worst form of death. Jesus Christ was crucified on the cross.

Yet, the world did not anticipate the Resurrection that followed such a public crucifixion. Jesus Christ defied the odds and rose again on the third day. He ascended into heaven and is seated at the Father's right hand (Mark 16:19).

We have access to the Father because of what Christ did for us. God has invited us back into His kingdom. We have access to everything God originally created and intended for humanity to enjoy. I want to shout at this! Yes, that should bring you joy. This news should delight your heart, knowing that the Father went to all this length so that you could have everything in His kingdom.

He calls

There was a significant moment in Jesus' ministry when He walked through Jericho and unexpectedly stopped under a sycamore fig tree, puzzling everyone around Him. People wondered what could have caught His attention on the tree, but Jesus knew what He was waiting for.

A short man named Zacchaeus had climbed up the tree to get

a better glimpse of Jesus passing by. But to his utter surprise, Jesus stopped right under the tree and called out his name. Jesus instructed Zacchaeus to come down immediately and invited Himself to dinner at Zacchaeus' house (Luke 19:1-10).

People did not particularly like Zacchaeus because he was a chief tax collector who had acquired his wealth through ill-gotten means. At that time, tax collectors were despised by the Jews because they abused their position to make more money from their people than they should, thereby increasing the poverty rate. So, Jesus stopping to speak to Zacchaeus seemed peculiar to those seeking His attention in the crowd.

On another occasion, Jesus and His disciples arrived in the town of Samaria. He sent them to buy food while He remained near Jacob's well. Unbeknownst to the disciples, Jesus orchestrated this moment to encounter a woman Bible scholars refer to as Photini. Jesus' interaction with this woman brought her restoration. She went from being a woman of ill repute, ashamed and ostracised to a woman who found her identity as a child of God, and through her, the whole of Samaria heard the good news of Christ (John 4:1-42).

To be singled out from the crowd is an extraordinary experience. That is what Jesus did amidst the chaos in the crowd. Just as Jesus paused in His day to call out and interact with these two individuals, He calls you to Himself. He invites you along on this journey so you will be a part of His kingdom. Just like Zacchaeus and Photini willingly responded to His invitation to a conversation and a relationship with Jesus, you should also be open to making the time and effort to respond to His call. In His kingdom, you will find a new sense of identity and security not based on wealth, marital status or societal labels. You can say with the Psalmist:

> *The Lord is my rock and my place of safety. He is the God who saves me. My God is my rock. I go to him for safety. He*

is like a shield to me. He's the power that saves me. He's my place of safety.

Psalm 18:2, NIRV

He knows

During the early years of my marriage, I experienced a deep sense of irrelevance and insignificance. I felt that my life held no exceptional value and that I had nothing meaningful to contribute. The words of King Solomon in Ecclesiastes, *"Life is meaningless,"* resonated deeply within me, leaving me feeling empty and unrecognised. I found myself in unfamiliar territory, surrounded by unfamiliar faces, struggling to fit in. Like the Samaritan woman by the well, I had tasted the bitter taste of life, and I longed for something more.

In the midst of my struggles, Psalm 139 became a lifeline for me. God revealed Himself to me in a tangible way, reminding me of my worth and value. He intimately knew every aspect of my life, understanding the words spoken over me by the world and the negative thoughts I had believed about myself.

Photini was shocked when she started quoting Jewish history to the strange man by the well, and it turned out Jesus knew her life history all along. Nothing was left untouched; her life was laid bare and He exposed her secrets to her.

Imagine how incredible it is to be known intimately by the Creator of the universe. He has chosen you and desires to be an active and essential part of your life. He values your thoughts, emotions, experiences, and words because you are significant to Him. He longs to be at the centre of your life and a part of every aspect of your being.

You are a masterpiece intricately created by the Father. You bring Him immense delight, and all the creatures in heaven are in awe of you. That is how much you are known and adored in heaven. Your creator has numbered every hair on your head. Everything about you brings Him great joy (Ephesians 2:10).

Perhaps life has placed labels on you that make you want to hide from the Father. Or maybe you have felt disconnected because life has a way of throwing challenges our way. But just as Jesus called Zacchaeus down from the tree, He is calling out to you today. He desires to spend time with you, not just some of your time but all of it, even for all of eternity. He longs to become a vital part of your life, flowing through every aspect of who you are.

Today, God is extending an invitation for you to come to Him. He has paused your day, saying, *"Come, let us reason together."* No matter what situation you find yourself in or where life has taken you, God wants to be an integral part of your daily life.

> *Come, let's talk this over, says the Lord; no matter how deep the stain of your sins, I can take it out and make you as clean as freshly fallen snow. Even if you are stained as red as crimson, I can make you white as wool.*
> **Isaiah 1:18, TLB**

Just as it was an ordinary day for Zacchaeus when he found himself perched atop the sycamore fig tree and a normal day for Photini by Jacob's well, today is your day. It is your moment, and God is personally calling you by name. He knows you intimately, and He desires to have a deep and meaningful relationship with you.

He is in it

The enemy deceived me with the lie that my voice held no significance. I believed that nobody cared to listen or hear my words. I believed that lie for so long, and I shut myself out. Whenever I spoke up and was shut down, I took it personally and agreed that the enemy was right and nobody wanted to hear my voice.

This lie silenced me in so many ways that it shut out everything until I heard this truth from God: **Everything within me is from Him. The person I am is because of Him. He made me who I am, and He made me this way, so everything that comes out of me pleases His heart.** That was a liberating point for me. And I believe that is what He is saying to you as well. God says that you are the apple of His eye. He wants to be a part of your life. He knows you, and He is in this with you.

The next time you feel like you are doing life on your own or you are so overwhelmed that there is no room for Jesus, I want you to know He is right there alongside you. He has been there the whole time. He wants to make Himself available to you. He wants to make Himself more present in your life. He wants you to be aware of His abiding presence in your everyday.

Whatever your day, life, or people have told you that you are or are not, you have or have not, or you can or cannot, know that the Father is in you. No matter how little or insignificant you think your work or contribution is, the Holy Spirit is right there with you. You have never been alone. Any thoughts or words that say otherwise are straight from hell and the enemy. That is his attempt to silence what is inside of you. You are valuable and essential; you are needed and matter now.

I know what it feels like to be a mom, a wife, or a worker. Your life is hectic and you do not seem to have any time to fit God into your daily schedule. I want you to know that God does not need you to fit Him into your life; He is already in there. He is already in your busy life. God wants you to know He has been right there with you in the busyness of taking care of your family, friends, and career. God is in there and wants to make you aware that He is in this with you.

The Bible says God knows even the number of hairs on your head (Luke 12:7). He knew you before birth and intricately formed you in your mother's womb. This is how intentional God was with you even before you were born. And He is inviting you to have that same intimate and intentional relationship with Him. He wants to be a part of who you are and what you do – what you think, feel, experience, say, and do. He wants to be in the essence of who you are; this is what He is offering you today.

Reel it in

Does all this sound too good to be true? Yeah, I would think the same if I were you, too. But step back and indulge with me for a little while. I want you to hang around beyond this chapter to hear a bit about how we get stuck in this presence and intimacy God is offering us.

It will come as no surprise to you that my second visa application was successful. There were no issues; we did not have to struggle or explain ourselves because we were legally married, and our marital relationship allowed me to access the United Kingdom.

Likewise, your relationship with God entitles you to many things you would not receive if you do not say, *"Yes, I do."* God is extending His invitation to a higher-level relationship with you that is way better than dating or courtship. He is calling you to be His beloved partner.

> *Israel, the Lord who created you says, "Do not be afraid—I will save you. I have called you by name—you are mine.*
>
> **Isaiah 43:1, GNT**

Like Jeremiah, God knew you before you were born.

> *Before I even formed you in your mother's womb, I knew all about you. Before you drew your first breath, I had already chosen you to be My prophet to speak My word to the nations.*
>
> **Jeremiah 1:5, VOICE**

He promises to be with you always.

> *"If you really love me, you will keep the commandments I have given you and I shall ask the Father to give you someone else to stand by you, to be with you always. I mean the Spirit of truth, whom the world cannot accept, for it can neither see nor recognise that Spirit. But you recognise him, for he is with you now and will be in your hearts. I am not going to leave you alone in the world—I am coming to you. In a very little while, the world will see me no more but you will see me, because I am really alive and you will be alive too. When that day come, you will realise that I am in my Father, that you are in me, and I am in you.*
>
> **John 14:15-20, PHILLIPS**

Time of Reflection

- ▶ What is one thing you have believed about God that is not from Him?
- ▶ How does it feel to know you have all the heavenly resources available to you?
- ▶ What is one thing you would do if you had the key that unlocks all doors?
- ▶ How does it feel to know God is giving you this key right now?

∞

Activation

Ask God to show you what He knows about you that is hidden from you. Just as He called Jeremiah to the nations, ask the Lord where He is calling you now in this season. Then, finally, offer to the Father any area of your life that seems remote from Him and ask Him to take over.

∞ ∞ ∞

Lord, you know everything there is to know about me. You perceive every movement of my heart and soul, and you understand my every thought before it even enters my mind.
Psalm 139:1-2, TPT

Two

Our Reality

Even if I go through the deepest darkness,
I will not be afraid, Lord, for you are
with me. Your shepherd's rod
and staff protect me.
Psalm 23:4, GNT

I cannot fully comprehend the emotions you are experiencing or the season of life you are currently in. However, I want to express how much I cherished being a wife. Simply being there for my husband brought me immense joy and fulfilment. Watching our family grow and evolve was a unique and beautiful experience. From just the two of us, we welcomed our first bundle of joy, turning us into a family of three. And a few years later, our family had expanded to five! Needless to say, we were kept quite busy.

However, at a certain point, reality hit us with full force. Suddenly, my responsibilities multiplied. Instead of cooking and caring for just two or three, I found myself catering to the needs of a family of five while juggling my work obligations. This relentless cycle drained me, and I struggled to maintain my enthusiasm and energy as a devoted mother.

To put it mildly, it has been exhausting and I lost much of the passion and motivation I once had for my home. To add to the challenge, our family had just moved to a new town where we knew hardly anyone. We did not anticipate getting any support, but at that moment, we felt it was part of God's plan for us. We were determined to invest a great deal into helping our family settle into our new community.

Amidst the incessant tantrums of a two-year-old boy who feels entitled to his tears and the nagging from a seven-year-old who cannot tolerate her five-year-old sister, we were not worried at all. It was more than just the kids who were having a brilliant time at being not-so-great. We also struggled to rely on and support each other through the tide as a couple.

I may, therefore sum it up as a very chaotic season with many highs and lows. Amidst it all, we were confident that God was on our side, that there was relief at the end of the tunnel, and that we would finally arrive.

With both of us in full-time job roles in different locations, our daily routine was anything but desirable. Ebenezer had to commute to London early in the morning and I had the responsibility of dropping off our children at various care settings before I could drive myself to my full-time job. Did I say that I had just started a new job? Oh yes! We had moved to this new town so I could pursue a new career while also bringing Ebenezer closer to his workplace. As the kids were at different ages and stages, they attended separate schools, resulting in me making three different drop-offs in three different locations before I could even begin my workday. Then, at the end of the day, it was the same hassle with multiple pickups to get everyone home. This made the trip for these drop-offs and pick-ups neither entertaining nor fascinating.

We mostly arrived home totally wiped out and desperate to get dinner out of the way so we could snuggle our tired bodies away. As you can imagine, dinner time was very stressful, and we had to make it work, trying to stay sane.

All I can say is that it was an incredibly demanding and strenuous period. We had no time to catch our breath, reflect, or engage in any meaningful activities. We were constantly tired, worn out, stressed, and completely drained within the confines of our little world. It felt like a never-ending cycle without any glimmer of hope for an end in sight.

Where did the time go?

You may be able to relate to my story even if your cycle may be spiralling with different activities from mine. Everyone goes through the busyness of life at different times and in varying states. Life is just plain busy; there is no time for the things that you define as meaningful to your life. Whether you are a single person or married and with a family, we are busy with stuff. Life has a way of taking all our time away, leaving us totally encumbered.

Do you realise that keeping busy comes quickly, and staying still is just too hard? It is much easier to find ourselves so busy with stuff than to try to stay still for a moment. I am not sure why, but that is the reality. That is life's way of robbing us of what we desperately need: our true selves.

You are not meant to be just a doer who keeps going. I often say that we are human beings; we have to BE first before we can DO. However, when we are busy and never stop, we do not have time to be still, peaceful, or present so that our bodies can get what we require before continuing. We labour ceaselessly.

Life tends to consume our time quickly and if we do not pause, take a seat, and make time work for us, we will discover that it always slips away from us and that we are always running out of it.

I often found myself in a state of constant demand, with various things vying for my time. I felt as though there was not enough time for anything, not even to read my Bible. I constantly asked, *"Where did the time go?"* It took a lot of falling and rising to reach the state of being intentional about simply being still.

Are you also always asking, *"Where did the time go?"* Do you find that you are always in a hurry, yet you do not seem to get enough done during the day?

I discovered two things in that season of my life. The first lesson was that I needed to be mindful that I am an individual, not just a wife, mother, employee and church member. Secondly, I needed to learn how to intentionally sit down with myself and give myself permission to be who I am, rest, be quiet, and navigate the chaos unfolding around me.

Learning to be intentional as an individual, wife, mother, employee, church member, and in my other responsibilities was the starting point of taking back control of my time. The word *"intentionality"* became a regular part of my vocabulary because I had to be intentional about choosing myself over everything else going on. I realised that I had to be intentional about making time for myself. ME time became a treasured part of my day.

Saying no to activities and pausing in my day so I could catch a breath, so I could just be still and let my body rejuvenate, settle down and be fed, was something that I prized dearly. God desires that you live a whole, productive and fruitful life, but He also desires that you learn how and when to be still.

Do not let time overtake and consume you because every day will end with, *"Where did the time go?"* Time will not stand still if you do not take care of yourself. Time will keep moving, and you will keep asking the same question. You cannot let time steal your life by taking everything from you.

I recently sat with God to read through this intriguing book of the Bible, Ecclesiastes. Solomon, the wisest and most incredible king ever known, penned these words. Solomon had it all: the wealth, the influence, the name—everything we keep dreaming of was available to this king, but he realised one day that all our pleasures are ultimately meaningless. What! Yes, Solomon had it all, yet he considered it all futile.

Life has interesting ways of phasing out all your experiences. The actual controller of your life is TIME. The real boss of your life is TIME. You have been dealt a measure of TIME and can only control the NOW version. What has already happened and what is yet to happen sit outside your radar and control. No matter how hard you try, you can never make the future turn out as you predicted or desired. You can only live and hope in the One who holds time in His hands.

But as for me, I trust in You, Lord, I say, "You are my God."
My times are in Your hand.
Psalm 31:14-15a, NASB

It is imperative that, whatever life looks like for you, you make time for yourself. Make time to sit still. Make time to reflect on your day. Make time to think about your words and your thought process.

There is a set time for everything and every activity under the sun, and our NOW called the PRESENT, is a gift to you. Make the most of it. You cannot change the past, and you cannot control the future, so offer the PRESENT to the Father so you can get all He has for you out of it. In the stillness, you can clearly hear what the Father is saying.

> *The Lord directs the steps of the godly. He delights in every detail of their lives.*
>
> **Psalms 37:23, NLT**

This starts by letting go of things that easily hold you down and making room for the new things He has for you daily. His mercies are renewed daily; you can get mercy for the day if you can spend your days with Him.

Race of life

I found something very fascinating going on in my life at a certain point. Everyone around me was caught up in busyness. Doing it all and giving it all because of the perception that you will be valued and accepted if you do. I fell into that trap as well. I signed up for everything that needed to be done and showed up for every meeting and every event.

I found that my life was mostly filled with activities that were not even things I enjoyed. I acted with other people's happiness or approval in mind. If you have been in my shoes before, you know exactly what that feels like. If you have not, then well done to you!

Recently, I learned from an influential woman of God about the *"man-pleasing spirit"* - the tendency to prioritise others' opinions over our own well-being. My life was encumbered with fulfilling roles and responsibilities I had burdened myself with, just like Martha did when Jesus came to her house in Bethany with his disciples. Mary, her sister, chose to sit with Jesus, but Martha was busy cooking and serving, consumed with creating an excellent atmosphere for her visitors. Martha must have been shocked when Jesus told her that sitting with Him was more important than being a great hostess (Luke 10:38-42).

A life of unending work, demands, and pressure, a life of positions, titles, and roles, comes in all forms. At first glance, it may not appear harmful, especially when we believe the work is good and necessary. But I found out recently that if you do not prioritise taking care of yourself as an individual, when you break down, all the tasks and events you thought were so important would remain uncompleted. It is better to leave some tasks undone in the short term while you take care of yourself, ensuring that you can be healthy and alive for the important things and people who need you in the long term.

Even Jesus and His disciples made time to rest and recharge after a long day of ministering to people. When the disciples returned to Nazareth after spending time preaching and ministering in nearby villages, Jesus immediately advised them to eat and rest, but instead, the community came to them for help. Every time Jesus suggested they leave, more people turned up. Eventually, after he had fed all those present, He instructed His disciples to leave and He left them to be alone in a secluded place (Mark 6).

I realised that a busy life did not benefit me in any way. Despite giving everything I had to all these diverse endeavours, I found myself miserable. I tried different things to find relief, but none of them truly helped because I consistently made poor choices and neglected my own well-being.

Fear of the future keeps us tethered to busyness, constantly feeling the need to be occupied and productive. Jesus warned His listeners:

> *"Therefore I tell you, do not worry about your life, what you will eat or drink; or about your body, what you will wear. Is not life more than food, and the body more than clothes? Look at the birds of the air; they do not sow or reap or store away in barns, and yet your heavenly Father feeds them. Are you not much more valuable than they? Can any one of you by worrying add a single hour to your life? "And why do you worry about clothes? See how the flowers of the field grow. They do not labor or spin. Yet I tell you that not even Solomon in all his splendor was dressed like one of these. If that is how God clothes the grass of the field, which is here today and tomorrow is thrown into the fire, will he not much more clothe you—you of little faith? So do not worry, saying, 'What shall we eat?' or 'What shall we drink?' or 'What shall we wear?' For the pagans run after all these things, and your heavenly Father knows that you need them. But seek first his kingdom and his righteousness, and all these things will be given to you as well. Therefore do not worry about tomorrow, for tomorrow will worry about itself. Each day has enough trouble of its own.*

> **Matthew 6:25-34, NIV**

Allow the Father, who knows tomorrow, to guide you in whatever you do so you can receive your great reward from Him. Let go of everything that threatens to take your peace and joy, allowing the Father to bring His divine guidance.

I encourage you to thoughtfully question why you prioritise the things you do. Are the things you do simply for the joy of it, or are they to make you feel accepted and included? Let everything you do be done for the Lord and not for men.

Whatever you do, work at it wholeheartedly as though you were doing it for the Lord and not merely for people. You know that it is from the Lord that you will receive the inheritance as a reward. It is the Lord Messiah whom you are serving!

Colossians 3:23-24, ISV

I pray that the Father's applause for your efforts will provide you with the motivation and desire in whatever you do now.

A piece of the pie

I mostly enjoy baking, and one thing I found enthralling is baking a dessert. Pavlova is my all-time good friend and favourite dessert that brings joy and delight to my soul.

Pavlova and I were first introduced at a work bring-and-share, and I fell in love. I chased my colleague down for the recipe and attempted a billion times to make it until, one day, Voila! I nailed it.

Anyone who has walked this path knows well that it takes a lot of effort to make it and pull it all together, but the most fantastic thing once it is all done and is ready to be served is the slicing. Having baked it well, you will be rewarded with a well-layered slice you can tuck in nicely.

There is never a crumb left on the plate after serving pavlova. That is what I find sobering about staring at the now empty plate; it looks like all my hard work is gone.

Consider how you desire a piece of pie when it is served. It makes you happy, but suddenly it all disappears. And that is how life might feel at times. Sometimes, life feels like you constantly give yourself away and dish out of your empty vessel. And even though you may feel satisfied, you soon realise that as you keep giving yourself away, you feel physically and emotionally drained. You believe serving others could make them feel good and pleased; however, doing so from an empty place only depletes you.

So, how can you continue to give yourself away without emptying the plate? Can you give slices of pavlova to the people you love and serve and still have some left for yourself? And still have the plates full? Only God can do that. Only God can ask you to serve others with your whole heart and still fill and make you complete.

> *"Come, all you who are thirsty. Come and drink the water I offer to you. You who do not have any money, come. Buy and eat the grain I give you. Come and buy wine and milk. You will not have to pay anything for it. Why spend money on what is not food? Why work for what does not satisfy you? Listen carefully to me. Then you will eat what is good. You will enjoy the richest food there is."*
> **Isaiah 55:1-2, NIRV**

Some time ago, I had an interesting experience. On this day, we went out in the morning and right in the middle of interacting with people, I suddenly realised how empty and lonely I was. I came home and stole some peace and quiet time while my kids were downstairs, immersed in their own worlds, and my lovely husband was outside in the garden, soaking up some sunshine.

I started reflecting on the events of that morning. How could I feel so lonely amidst a buzzing crowd? All the pains of my life, all the hurt I had experienced, all played before me, and all I could see was a hopeless life for me in that minute of silence.

I cried as I lay on my bed. The weight of the pain in my chest was beating so hard at me. It was pulling my lungs apart. It was taking the life out of me. All I felt at that moment was emptiness and darkness.

And as I lay there, the pictures I saw of my future life did not give me any hope or peace. It was such a surreal moment; it felt like time stood still, and suddenly, I was all alone in this world.

I was alone in my room, with my life playing before me. I was desperate and asked questions like these. *"How can this be the life you have called for me? Did you send me here for this kind of life? Can anything good come out of this?"* I asked for help, and with my wild imagination, I hoped that instantly, thunder would strike and the roof on top of my house would open up. I was desperate to see or hear something unusual happen, like in some stories I had heard.

At this moment, I stumbled upon a sermon by a dear woman who compared my life experience to a maze. You may understand it better if you have ever found yourself in one. A maze has no clear path but has many routes, and figuring out how to get to the exit can take tremendous effort.

Most of the time, depending on your confidence and navigational skills, you may make it out quickly; however, if your navigational skills are not up to scratch, it may seem like you've been lost for a long time. Worse still, you may need another person to help you figure out how to get out.

Your life may be feeling like a maze with several unexpected turns, and trying to understand everything happening to you can seem overwhelming. For me, the reality of being so alone in my world drove me to my knees.

I realised I needed someone to help me navigate my way out of this maze. So, with tears streaming down my face, I surrendered my life to God. I found His voice in His words, saying, *"I will help you. I will take you through it. Just hold my hand, and I will take you where you need to go."*

At that moment, even though the heaviness and emptiness were still there and everything in my surroundings was still the same, something had changed inside me. A light had been shown inside me. Now I knew what to do and who would take me through this. I knew in that instant who would be my support system and the one I could rely on.

The next stage of my life was a real journey. I developed the habit of returning to my Maker for replenishment whenever I felt physically and emotionally drained, seeking Him to recharge me so I could continue to give to others. I used to be the one who readily offered help even when I was exhausted or struggling to make ends meet. Unfortunately, this often made me feel lonely because I neglected to prioritise self-care and self-love, which only made me more miserable. I took Jesus' advice and returned to drink from His fountain of endless life:

> *Jesus answered, "If you drink from Jacob's well, you'll be thirsty again, but if anyone drinks the living water I give them, they will never be thirsty again. For when you drink the water I give you, it becomes a gushing fountain of the Holy Spirit, flooding you with endless life!"*
>
> **John 4:13-14, TPT**

I learnt to wait for Jesus to fill me and make me whole before I poured myself out. Suppose your life is anything like what I have described, then the emptiness and loneliness you feel after serving others can only be filled by Him and satisfied by Him.

Reel it in

Something is always going on in life, and if you do not take the time to sit quietly and receive from the Father, you will find yourself burned out and out of it. If your life is hectic and overwhelming, it is important to take a moment to be still and allow the love of the Father to wash over you. This will renew and rejuvenate you, giving you the strength to face each day as it comes.

> *The steadfast love of the Lord never ceases; his mercies never come to an end; they are new every morning; great is your faithfulness.*
>
> **Lamentations 3:22-23, ESV**

Living a hectic life can prevent you from focusing on what truly matters. However, by letting go of anything that holds you back, you can create space within yourself to allow the presence of the Father to fill you up. This will enable you to pour into the lives of others.

> *As for us, we have all of these great witnesses who encircle us like clouds. So we must let go of every wound that has pierced us and the sin we so easily fall into. Then we will be able to run life's marathon race with passion and determination, for the path has been already marked out before us. We look away from the natural realm and we focus our attention and expectation onto Jesus who birthed faith within us and who leads us forward into faith's perfection. His example is this: Because his heart was focused on the joy of knowing that you would be his, he endured the agony of the cross and conquered its humiliation, and now sits exalted at the right hand of the throne of God! So consider*

carefully how Jesus faced such intense opposition from sinners who opposed their own souls, so that you won't become worn down and cave in under life's pressures.

Hebrews 12:1-3, TPT

God desires to occupy all of your time with Himself. Instead of letting life overwhelm you, let God fill you with Himself.

May God himself, the God who makes everything holy and whole, make you holy and whole, put you together—spirit, soul, and body—and keep you fit for the coming of our Master, Jesus Christ. The one who called you is completely dependable. If he said it, he'll do it!

1 Thessalonians 5:23-24, MSG

Time of Reflection

- Why do you do the things that you do?
- Who are you pleasing most in all these activities, roles and responsibilities?
- Who is genuinely benefiting from the things you do?
- If it does not add value to your life, ask yourself, is it worth doing?
- If you let it go, could someone who is best suited for it take over so that you have free time on your hands to do things that you genuinely enjoy doing?

Activation

Intentionally create time this week and clear up your calendar so you can sit silently for at least half an hour each day. Find a quiet space, bring a pen and notepad, and write down everything that comes to mind. You could draw or write whatever that looks like. Now, ask God what that means and ask Him to guide and support you in clearing away anything consuming your time so that you have time for the things that are truly important in your life.

∞∞∞

You discern my going out and my lying
down; you are familiar with all my ways.
Psalm 139:3, NIV

Three

The Table is Set

He takes me to lush pastures,
he leads me to refreshing water.
Psalm 23:2, NET

In the midst of my overflowing excitement upon finally receiving the visa to start my new life with my love, the thought of leaving Ghana consumed my mind. The joy of finally being with my husband overshadowed any ounce of sorrow or regret for leaving my family behind.

It is a dream come true for any newlywed young woman to finally be with her Mr. Man, and that was all I felt. Our families were excited for us as they waved goodbye at the airport. There was so much joy and peace as we discussed the life that awaited us in the UK.

It was not until we boarded the aeroplane and were up in the soaring skies that I had a minute to think through the events of my life over the previous few days. As I sat beside him, holding hands and doing my best to avoid his gaze, it finally struck me which path I had taken.

Suddenly, a rush of thoughts overwhelmed me: *"What have I gotten myself into? I am leaving with this man, leaving everything I have ever known behind."* In that moment, a flood of emotions surged within me, and tears streamed down my face.

He looked at me lovingly and tenderly as if he understood my pain. He clung to my hand and said, *"We are going to be alright,"* and I believed him. There was no way I could predict how that was going to work since I had no idea where he was taking me.

Throughout the remainder of the journey, my husband shared his experiences and painted a picture of our new life together. The excitement returned, and I couldn't wait to embark on this journey by his side.

As we arrived at Gatwick Airport, everything was utterly perplexing. London was nothing like I expected. It was a bizarre and exhilarating feeling.

After some errand-running, we eventually reached our first new house. Even though it was merely a basic accommodation, it felt like bliss – an extraordinary place where we could begin our life together. The first night, his friend offered us a place to stay until we gained all the essentials to start our new life in our new home.

I had to get used to this new place and our new life as husband and wife for the first few months. I found the surroundings and individuals I met and being a part of a new family and community intriguing as I tried to make sense of it all.

When I began job-hunting, life in the UK had something else for me. I was sad to realise I could not work in my chosen field. Regrettably, I had to choose a completely different field.

I formed some beautiful friendships and connections, which were all loving and healthy. Our marriage was beautiful even though we had our fair share of difficulties adjusting to living together for the first time.

Over the first few years, several of the relationships I had established grew stale. Private conversations ended up in the public domain, leading to a very messy situation that left people hurt. In my devastation, I prayed for the earth to swallow me, but since earthquakes never happen when people command it to, I endured the shame, ridicule, and name-calling that followed.

It was an experience that no one could have prepared me for. I felt lost and tried my hardest to find my way out. I attempted some churches nearby, but nothing seemed to take my pain away or lead me to the God who could save me. I was just dead inside. I tried to find God by reading the Bible multiple times, but unfortunately, I could not find Him. He seemed to be absent. I went to several church events and prayed as much as possible, but all to no avail.

It felt like a defenceless rabbit in a jungle, surrounded by gnawing and gnarling predators, ready to devour this guilty prey with no hope for and no expectation of survival. I thought that would be the end of me. But this was not the end of my story. Life had more in store for me.

All you need is here

When God sets a table for you, no one can unset it. No one can alter what God has specifically prepared for you. He knows your situation, understands exactly what you require, and customizes a table to fulfil your needs.

This is the nature of our Heavenly Father. He lavishly sets a table before you, overflowing with everything you could ever require. Therefore, any circumstance or perception in your life that suggests lack or insufficiency is nothing more than a false narrative.

Everything you need to survive, succeed in life, and live abundantly has already been prepared for you. It is accessible and available to you now. Remember, you are more than enough for every challenge that comes your way. You have the ability to overcome any challenge you face.

> *You can be sure that God will take care of everything you need, his generosity exceeding even yours in the glory that pours from Jesus. Our God and Father abounds in glory that just pours out into eternity. Yes.*
>
> **Philippians 4:19-20, MSG**

I once longed for connection, to feel something meaningful in my life, and to see the evidence of my efforts. Unfortunately, my environment did not provide that nourishment for me.

What is your environment feeding you? When you look in the mirror, what story do you see reflected back at you? Or maybe your life is constantly busy, and while you make time for God here and there, you have yet to experience true fulfilment and wholeness within yourself.

Today, God is telling you that everything you need is right here, right now. He is the source of your life. The Father has made available everything you need to lead a purposeful and fruitful life, and He desires that for you. No matter what your life looks like, God is inviting Himself in. He is opening the doors to your heart so that you may see Him clearly. He has always been there, and you can have access to Him.

The Lord is near to everyone who prays to him, to every faithful person who prays to him.

Psalm 145:18, GW

There is a story in the Bible about Elisha and a widow (2 Kings 4:1–7). This woman was a widowed wife of one of the sons of the prophets. She told Elisha her husband was dead and the creditor was about to take her sons away.

And Elisha said to her, "What shall I do for you? Tell me; what have you in the house?" And she said, "Your servant has nothing in the house except a jar of oil."

2 Kings 4:2, ESV .

To her, it was an empty place. All she could see was a jar of oil. However, Elisha saw from a different place, so what he told her made little sense to the natural mind. It would have sounded unbelievable and ridiculous.

Then he said, "Go, borrow vessels from everywhere, from all your neighbors—empty vessels; do not gather just a few. And when you have come in, you shall shut the door behind you and your sons; then pour it into all those vessels, and set aside the full ones."

2 Kings 4:3-4, NKJV

She hurriedly sent her sons to ask around the village and bring them to her. They borrowed as many empty vessels as they could find, came in, and shut the door as Elisha had instructed. Then she poured until they had filled up all the vessels.

From a small jar of oil, she found herself blessed with an abundance that allowed her to settle her husband's debts and secure her sons' future. Can you relate to the widow's plight? I, too, have often found myself in that very position. I look at my seemingly barren life, and all I see is emptiness; I have often thought there is nothing good that could come out of this life.

However, God enters my life and fills it up, just like He did with the widow. From her meagre supply of oil, vessels that liberated others became her narrative. She could have wandered off to find solace in her neighbours or begged her creditors, but nobody could have done the miracle she and her sons had witnessed.

When you look at your own life, you may feel a sense of emptiness. You may feel you have nothing. Yet God is saying that everything you need is right here because He can make it work. He is able to make everything materialise in your life for you. God can turn things around and cause your life to move in its intended direction. You have to let Him in so He can be there for you. To fully experience this transformation, you must invite Him in, opening the door and creating space for His presence. For it is within Him that you will discover everything you need to thrive.

> God can pour on the blessings in astonishing ways so that you're ready for anything and everything, more than just ready to do what needs to be done. As one psalmist puts it: He throws caution to the winds, giving to the needy in reckless abandon. His right-living, right-giving ways never run out, never wear out. This most generous God who gives seed to the farmer that becomes bread for your meals is more than extravagant with you. He gives you something you can then give away, which grows into full-formed lives, robust in God, wealthy in every way, so that you can be generous in every way, producing with us great praise to God.
>
> **2 Corinthians 9:8-11, MSG**

The remarkable thing is that I was unaware that there was even a remote possibility that God was present in my life. My existence was consumed by the debris of clutter and it seemed that God was distant, beyond reach. Due to my perception of God as the righteous being He is, I held no hope that He would ever grace my life with His presence.

Yet that was precisely the gift He gave me. God led me to this place and revealed that He had been there all along, faithfully standing by my side. And this is the message He imparts to you as well. God does not ask us to become perfect, to become right, to get our acts together, to get everything in place and in line before He can come and be in our lives.

Consider the story of Cain and Abel if you are familiar with it. Even after Cain's actions, God still reached out to him. God appeared to him. Such is the nature of our God - always present, always reaching out to us, delighting in being with us and speaking to us.

You might be surprised to learn that for the longest time, I unconsciously had inner conversations with myself. It was quite embarrassing until God revealed to me that it was actually Him speaking to me. The thoughts that danced through my mind were not ramblings of madness but rather the profound work of the Holy Spirit, communicating with me without my awareness.

If you have ever found yourself talking to yourself, whispering thoughts, know that is your spirit engaging with the Spirit of God.

I must emphasise that when God's thoughts manifest in your mind, they are always good. He never speaks evil or negativity towards us, because He is a good God and only has good intentions for us.

When you have thoughts that do not align with the character of God, you can recognise that they are coming from a different source, and you need to firmly reject them. The enemy enjoys filling our minds with deceitful lies and falsehoods. He delights in distorting situations with a twisted perspective to keep us bound.

However, the Holy Spirit continues to diligently work within us, empowering us to live in freedom according to God's desires and purposes. He longs to see your mind, heart and life set free so that you have an overflowing abundance that can be poured into the lives of others.

> *The Lord is the Spirit. And where the Spirit of the Lord is, there is freedom.*
>
> **2 Corinthians 3:17, ICB**

If, like me, you have ever found yourself in a challenging situation or felt distant from God, overwhelmed by the busyness of life, I want to assure you that God is right by your side. He has always been there, never once abandoning you.

Can this satisfy?

Have you ever found yourself in a crowded grocery store on a Saturday afternoon with your family, if you are a family of five like us? Your shopping cart is filled with everything you need for the week, and you're waiting in a long line at the checkout.

As you stand there, you cannot help but notice the family ahead of you. Maybe, like me, you are naturally curious about what others are buying. Sometimes, you find yourself admiring their purchases and wondering what they are going to cook. Maybe you even consider if it would be better for your own meals.

There is a tendency to draw inspiration from the actions of others. I have personally struggled with this same curiosity and inspiration when it comes to my relationship with God. Everyone seemed to do it differently. People expressed their faith in various ways. Some prayed fervently, while others prayed less. Some attended church regularly. It was confusing.

I had yet to figure out the best approach. This uncertainty contributed to my feelings of hopelessness as I sought God. It was overwhelming and confusing trying to figure out the *"right"* way to connect with God and find satisfaction in my faith.

What was enough, and what could bring me ultimate satisfaction? I used to believe that praying more would solve my problems, but unfortunately, it did not. Similarly, I thought that reading the Bible regularly would bring me closer to God, but it did not seem to have the desired effect.

Have you ever felt unsure of what you are supposed to be doing with God? It can be challenging, especially when you see others at church passionately praising and worshipping God while feeling disconnected yourself. You might wonder, *"How do they get to that place?"*

The pressure of not knowing how to connect with God can actually keep us further away from Him. But during my journey, I learned that God hasn't set a specific method for connecting with Him. He created each of us with unique abilities, talents, and preferences. Therefore, how we choose to serve and worship God should be personalized and authentic to who we are.

For example, my husband and I have different prayer styles and preferences, yet we both walk away from our times with God feeling satisfied. It's about finding what works for you and allowing God's Spirit to guide you.

God wants to release you from the pressure of fitting into a certain mould or following what others are doing. When you open yourself up to Him, you will be following His Spirit, not trying to copy someone else's actions.

Sometimes, all you need is to read a single Bible passage or meditating on one verse, and that may be enough for your spirit for the week. God doesn't require us to check boxes or follow rigid study plans just to feel a sense of accomplishment.

If you want your heart to be intimate and filled with the Spirit of God, allow His Spirit to lead you in how to express that intimacy. After spending time with God, you won't leave feeling guilty, even if it seems like you didn't receive much. You will eventually realize that it was more than enough for your spirit, as God knows your needs and how to meet them.

Connecting with God does not mean you have to stop your whole life. As a mother, I have found that I can connect with God even while doing household chores, like washing dishes or in the midst of a busy day. I make time in the morning for devoted prayer because it works for me. Find what works for you by allowing your heart to flow with Him. It all starts with your heart and the posture of openness and willingness to let your thoughts and emotions flow. That is how you will be filled. You know that your connection to the Father will cause satisfaction from which you will receive all the fulfilment you require as He flows into and fills you.

Comparing your connection with God to someone else's will only lead to frustration and dissatisfaction. You are unique and what works for someone else may not work for you. Instead, seek an intimate relationship with God where His Spirit fills and satisfies you.

I know many people who have studied the Bible for an entire year but didn't gain anything meaningful from it. That is not what God wants for you. There's more to seek than just the physical satisfaction of completing the Bible-in-a-year plan.

So, let go of expectations and open your heart to the leading of His Spirit. Allow Him to define how you connect with Him and find the deep fulfilment only He can provide.

His food makes whole

Do you find it fascinating to observe people who are free-spirited and fearless, seizing every opportunity that comes their way? They let nothing hold them back. They have similar circumstances and potential as you, but they embrace life without hesitation and they seize those chances.

Have you ever found yourself in a situation where you feel intimidated and out of your depth? Do you ever think that you are incapable of handling what is presented before you? Does the word *"cannot"* seem to dominate your thoughts and decisions, causing you to miss out on potential opportunities?

If you have ever been in that place, I want you to know that God wants to help you overcome it and experience wholeness. He wants to make you fearless and free, just like carefree children who believe they can do anything. When they spill juice on the floor, they think they can clean it up themselves without fear or limitation. When you were young, nothing held you back until the world defined what is possible and what isn't.

But the Spirit of God wants that kind of unrestricted perspective for you. He says that you can do all things. Do you know why? Because He is in you and He is for you.

> *I can do everything God asks me to with the help of Christ who gives me the strength and power.*
>
> **Philippians 4:13, TLB**

David could face the giant that terrified everybody else because he had had an encounter with the Lord. When nobody was watching, when he was tucked away in a field, tending his flock, he experienced the Spirit of God. God showed him what he could do when he placed his trust in Him. That is why he did not miss a beat when he faced that giant. David knew it was not up to him to do anything. It was all on God to make it happen.

How would you feel if the very thing you have been scared to do, the same thing you believed you couldn't do, suddenly became possible for you? How will that make you feel? God is offering you liberation. He's offering you the ability to break through and not let anything hold you back.

That does not mean you would not encounter lies and negativity that try to restrain you. They will always be there. But when the Spirit of God is leading and guiding your life, no matter what the enemy says, the Spirit of God will flow and give you the wisdom to overcome and do what needs to be done.

God wants to make you whole and fill you with His fullness. You can step into any situation and accomplish what needs to be done.

When God created Adam and Eve, they were fearless and unrestricted. They had everything they needed, and there were no limitations. But when they turned away from God, they encountered fear, anxiety, and depression. They began to hold on to things instead of embracing their freedom.

Ironically, what keeps us bound can also set us free. It is the spirit of control. Our human nature desires to control situations; we want to control narratives and outcomes. But holding on to that control only keeps us captive.

When you find yourself unable to control the outcome of a situation, fear, confinement, and restriction take over. However, when you relinquish control and surrender the circumstance to God, those things lose their hold on you.

Many times, we have held ourselves back because we've tried to tightly control the outcomes we believe are best for us. But God is asking you to let go. Let go of yourself and let Him take over. When you let go, you can receive what He has to offer you.

God offers you His protection and guidance. He provides everything you need to navigate through what you've been trying to control.

Considering I am a non-swimmer, I am out of league saying this, but what I discovered from my swimming lessons was that if you let go and trust the water, you set yourself free for the water to carry you, and then you can glide with ease. But if you cling tightly to your fear of drowning, you will weigh yourself down and begin to sink.

That is precisely what God wants you to do. He wants you to let go of whatever you feel entitled to. Let go of the future that you desperately desire. Let go of the plans and thoughts you have orchestrated for yourself and let Him take charge.

When God takes over, it will be perfect because His thoughts are always good. His plans for you are good and will give you a future and hope. When God narrates your story, it will end well.

Every day, give God whatever is troubling you, whether it is a problem in your family, job, or relationships. Visualise yourself entrusting those worries to Him. Instead of letting those concerns overwhelm you and consume your thoughts, release them to God.

Start allowing God to take control, and you'll experience the freedom of your spirit. You will see how unburdened and free you can be.

Soon, you will walk through life and realise you are not carrying heavy burdens. You would not harbour anger and unforgiveness because you have allowed God to be your vindicator. Let Him fight your battles for you. Let Him win for you.

When you have God on your side, advocating and fighting for you, there is no need for you to defend yourself because He becomes your ultimate defender.

A prime example of this is seen in the life of David, who faced numerous trials and even the threat of death from King Saul. Instead of taking matters into his own hands, David chose to entrust his battle to God, allowing Him to handle the situation. And as expected, God intervened, protected David, and ensured that the timing for his ascent to the throne was perfect.

Likewise, invite God to take care of every aspect of your life. Allow His healing power to restore you, and let His love make you whole. Surrender to His divine plan and timing, trusting that He knows what is best for you.

Reel it in

When I found myself in a deep hole in our community, God brought a light into my life at just the right time. He came to me and revealed who I truly am. Eventually, we found a wonderful church where I experienced fellowship with amazing people. Through this, I rediscovered myself and God became alive in my life.

God also brought a family into my life, a woman who was a powerful and beautiful voice for Him. She reminded me of myself and in my moments of feeling lost, God found me and helped me uncover my true identity. He restored my spirit, helped me rebuild my life, and I surrendered myself completely to Him.

However, this did not mark the end of all problems and challenges. I still found myself in difficult situations. The adversary continued to hurl darts in my direction, but he could not bring me down. I had built some resilience and had the backing of heaven and the people God had brought into my life.

God continued to bring uplifting individuals who supported me in maintaining my peace and bringing light back into my life. I was able to think positively and clearly, and through it all, I recognized myself.

Remember, your heavenly Father, who created the universe, is on your side. He wants to provide everything you need to live a victorious life.

> *What shall we say about such wonderful things as these? If God is for us, who can ever be against us? Since he did not spare even his own Son but gave him up for us all, won't he also give us everything else? Who dares accuse us whom God has chosen for his own? No one—for God himself has given us right standing with himself. Who then will condemn us? No one—for Christ Jesus died for us and was raised to life for us, and he is sitting in the place of honor at God's right hand, pleading for us.*
>
> **Romans 8:32-34, NLT**

God knows exactly what you need and can provide it to you. Allow Him to lead and guide you into all His truths concerning you.

> *I will instruct you (says the Lord) and guide you along the best pathway for your life; I will advise you and watch your progress.*
>
> **Psalm 32:8, TLB**

You must completely abandon yourself to God for Him to take control of your life and guide you to everything He created for you. God has laid out your entire future before you and knows the best way to get you there.

> *Trust in the Lord completely, and do not rely on your own opinions. With all your heart rely on him to guide you, and he will lead you in every decision you make. Become intimate with him in whatever you do, and he will lead you wherever you go.*
>
> **Proverbs 3:5-6, TPT**

Time of Reflection

- ▶ What is one lie you have believed that has affected your life?
- ▶ Can you easily forgive and allow God to be your vindicator?
- ▶ What are you holding on to that God asks you to let go of?
- ▶ Can you trust God that He knows best and can lead you to the best places for you?

Activation

Over the next few days, I encourage you to be mindful of every negative word that enters your mind or leaves your lips. Take note of them, and at the end of each day, seek God's guidance as to why these words have surfaced. Ask Him to replace those negative words with His truth. This exercise is meant to help you dig out the root of negativity in your life.

In addition, I suggest committing Philippians 4:8 to memory in your preferred Bible translation. This powerful verse reminds us to focus on thoughts that are true, honourable, just, pure, lovely, commendable, excellent, and praiseworthy. By internalizing this scripture, you will be equipped to shift your mindset towards positivity and align your thoughts with God's truth.

Together, these practices will help you cultivate a more positive and discerning mindset, enabling you to uproot negativity and embrace the transformative power of God's word in your life.

∞∞∞

You are so intimately aware of me, Lord.
You read my heart like an open book and
you know all the words I'm about to speak
before I even start a sentence! You know
every step I will take before my
journey even begins.
Psalm 139:3-4, TPT

Four

Feasting

You serve me a six-course dinner
right in front of my enemies.
Psalm 23:5, MSG

L ife presents us with numerous choices. As individuals, we can choose what we want to eat, what we want to wear, where we want to go, and even how we want to get there. Unlike robots, programmed to act a certain way, we possess the ability to explore different domains and embrace new beginnings.

An opportunity arose for us to embark on a fresh start when Ebenezer, driven by his aspiration to become the system architect he had always dreamed of, desired to pursue his career option. This decision was met with a mix of sadness and uncertainty as we bid farewell to the life we had known during the first few years of our marriage.

It was a life decision that only a few dared make in our circle, and you got little support if you ventured into that space. It was considered easy to live the life we had then, and anyone who stepped outside the boat faced many unknown and unfounded factors.

Therefore, making this decision was such a big deal. We knew we had a lot to lose, and there was no guarantee of sunshine at the end of this flight. Regrettably, we failed to seek God's guidance and wisdom in this matter.

Fortunately, we got tremendous support from a moving company, making the transition less burdensome as they efficiently packed and transported our belongings to our new home. What more could we ask for? We set off for our new home in our car, packed with our two-year-old.

It did not feel daunting or overwhelming this time because I had built some tenacity and resilience. We held onto the hope that our new beginning would be filled with promise and greatness. Ebenezer would undertake his Master's degree, and I would follow him after I finished all the mothering I had to do. Well, that was the plan.

In this new place, it was just a family we knew; they were superb with us. They connected us with other people as well, which was really lovely. It all felt very special. As it was an early start, we had little financial support, but that was not a problem. We had more than enough to survive and live on. I managed to find another menial job. Meanwhile, Ebenezer balanced his studies with evening work and the daily commute between university and home.

Then, out of the blue, I found out I was pregnant with my second daughter. It was an unexpected surprise for us, as we had not planned to raise another child since we had just begun our new life. All we wanted was to settle in and feel secure before thinking about it.

Well, people who have experienced these unexpected visitors will tell you that it can take a lot of mental adjustment to get used to and that is why we are grateful to nature for granting us a nine-month waiting period before our bundles of joy made their earthly appearances. And yes, I am one of those with a fun relationship with pregnancies; we do not really get along. Accordingly, when this came, that was precisely what it turned out to be: an abrupt interruption to our already cluttered lives. But we sailed through, and she came in November with all her glory—my pride and joy.

Her appearance paved the way for us to connect with our church community. They graciously supported us after her birth and dedication and we developed deep relationships with the people around us. We were eager to build connections, foster relationships, and find purpose in our lives. The church community embraced us wholeheartedly, making us feel welcome and at home. Eager to contribute, we readily offered our help wherever it was needed.

As time passed, the church decided to relocate its meeting venue closer to our home, allowing us to deeply immerse ourselves even more in the community. We were right in it, mainly the first ones to turn up to set it all up and ensure everything was going well, and then we mostly stayed behind, cleared it all up, and packed it away. This level of involvement initially brought us great joy and fulfilment.

However, over time, the initial excitement began to fade as we felt the weight of our responsibilities. We found ourselves leading various aspects of the church and bearing significant responsibilities. Without intending to, we had become the main driving force behind much of the community's activities, and our names became synonymous with the church. The joy we once felt started to diminish.

Eventually, we found ourselves in a place where we realised that the buzz was gone, the lights were out, the butterflies were not flying, and the juice had dried out in both of us. What had begun as a genuine desire to be part of something great and positively impact others had turned sour. The joy of serving had disappeared, leaving us feeling drained and questioning our purpose.

We realised that our eagerness to serve had been driven by a desire for approval and acceptance. We sought validation through our acts of service, hoping that by giving and committing ourselves fully, we would gain acceptance. However, no matter how much we poured into the community, it never seemed to fill the void within us.

Attending various church programs had become mundane, leaving us dissatisfied and disconnected. We recognized that this was not the fulfilling life we were meant to live – something needed to change. We made the difficult choice to step back, reevaluate our priorities, and let go of the need for constant busyness and approval.

In this moment of realisation, we understood that seeking the approval of others was a fruitless endeavour. We recognised that true fulfilment could only come from seeking to please one person: God. Rather than striving to gain recognition from others, we learned to focus on how God sees us – exactly as we are. Our actions should be directed towards honouring Him alone.

Therefore, we made the courageous decision to relinquish control and allow others to take up the responsibilities we had shouldered. Although it disappointed some, we felt an immense sense of relief, knowing deep down that it was the right choice. By doing so, we discovered the importance of living a life that pleases God alone. We embraced the realisation that our actions and decisions should be rooted in a genuine desire to honour Him rather than seeking validation from others.

From that point on, we dedicated ourselves to living a life that aligned with God's purpose for us. We sought His guidance and direction, finding freedom and purpose in living authentically for Him. Our involvement in the church became more intentional, focusing on utilising our gifts and talents where they were truly needed.

Reflecting on our journey and the multitude of responsibilities we had taken on, we realised that we had lost sight of who we truly were. We had allowed our lives to become filled with various obligations, overshadowing our authentic identities. In this realisation, we recognised the importance of aligning our actions with God's purpose rather than pursuing recognition from others.

Life, with all its choices and challenges, became an opportunity for growth and alignment with God's will. We became intentional about living a life directed by His guidance and devoted to His purpose. By letting go of our need for external approval, we found a renewed sense of purpose and a deeper connection with God.

Through this journey, we learned the significance of seeking God's approval above all else. We discovered that true fulfilment comes from aligning our actions with His will rather than constantly seeking validation from others. Let us remember to seek guidance and approval from God in every decision we make, for He alone holds the key to a purposeful and meaningful life.

How much can I have?

Now, the table has been set, and everything has been laid bare before you. You have been offered all the necessary nutrients. It is now up to you to feast on what has been served. You may find yourself thinking, *"I have received all this, so why am I not taking full advantage of it?"*

Something else is at play here. All the lies that have been told you may be holding you back, and because of that, you are not able to eat as much as you can. You are unable to enjoy everything that has been set before you.

These lies are deceptive, tricking us with words that throw us off guard. They are wrapped in forms like these: *"You are not enough. You don't deserve it. You are not welcome here. We don't want you."* If you look back on your life, the only time and place you hear such words being thrown at you and such narratives coming to you is in stifling environments. That is how you know they are straight from the enemy's camp in hell.

It is important to remember that everything in you, everything you have going on, is perfect because God created you in His complete perfection. When He made you, there was nothing wrong with you. There was nothing out of place about you. Everything about you was put in there exactly as God wanted. Unfortunately, like in my own story, we often carry more than we should. We become desperate for people to notice us, to see us, and to include us in community conversations. However, in pursuing validation from others, we lose ourselves in the process.

When you place your trust in God to care for you, He will pour into you all that you need. You must refuse the lies of the enemy that state that you are not enough, you are not valuable, and you are not accepted. None of that matters when God is the one shaping your narrative.

Whatever state of life you are in, there is a place hungry and desperate for your voice, for what you have to say, and what you have to offer. If you find yourself in circumstances where you are belittled or your efforts are falling on stony ground, take a step back and talk to God about it.

My spouse Ebenezer and I have had to do this many times. We

have been in places where we had to ask God, *"Do we need to be here?"* He will say, *"Stay!"* There are times and seasons in our lives when we have asked Him, *"Do we need to be here?"* and He will say, *"It's time to go."* We have had to make those difficult decisions. But you can only get there and know what He desires for you when you spend time with him.

Therefore, refuse to spend time in such negative energy and places and live a life free of self-pity, self-doubt, and insecurity. Disassociate yourself whenever you find yourself in a situation where you are marginalised or undervalued.

Every human being deserves to be loved. We are created with a need for love and acceptance. God has somebody out there who values you, accepts you, and is eager for what you have to offer. That is why you discover that partners in marriages complement one another. They are reliant and dependent on each other. Every sustainable and fruitful marriage is birthed by people who complement and rely on each other.

That is precisely the life that God has destined for you. You are incredibly valuable, and the world needs you, regardless of your background, talents, or the depths within you. The world needs to hear your voice and discover what resides within you. Don't allow your environment to hold you back. Allow God to set you free and make you whole. Allow God to release you to walk in the fullness of who you are.

Joseph started as a servant in the king's palace, then became a prisoner. The next thing he knew, he was the prime minister. The lies put on him were shaken off once the Spirit of God positioned him in his place of value.

There is a place for you. Do not waste time dwelling on your shortcomings or doubting your abilities as time goes by. While you wait for your opportunity and what God has in store for you, equip yourself, build yourself up, and spend time with the Spirit of God. Allow Him to teach you His ways and guide you towards what He has prepared specifically for you. You shouldn't wait for a person to hand you an opportunity when God has so much more in store for you.

Wake up, oh sleeping lion. Rise up and roar! Wake up and take your place. Wake up and do what you were born and destined to do. You are more than enough. You have more than enough and have what it takes to do what you need.

> *Moreover, we know that to those who love God, who are called according to his plan, everything that happens fits into a pattern for good. God, in his foreknowledge, chose them to bear the family likeness of his Son, that he might be the eldest of a family of many brothers. He chose them long ago; when the time came he called them, he made them righteous in his sight, and then lifted them to the splendour of life as his own sons.*
>
> **Romans 8:28-30, PHILLIPS**

Just as a potter moulds and shapes clay, the Father is moulding and shaping you. He is perfecting you and preparing you for your place of destiny. When He positions you exactly where He wants you, everything that flows out of you will be perfect and exactly what He needs you to be doing.

How do I take it?

Now that we know what it takes to do what God has assigned us, how do we build ourselves? How do we sustain the Spirit of God flowing through us? How do we ensure that what we feed ourselves is building us and not just staying redundant? God connects with us in different ways and forms; that is just the multifaceted God we serve.

When Jesus' disciples asked him, *"Can you teach us to pray? We see you pray a lot."* Jesus took them through the Lord's Prayer. It was as simple as that. In that prayer, He acknowledged the Lord as the Supreme Father, who reigns on the earth and in the heavens, and then offered the day to Him.

Therefore, I encourage you to begin by committing to giving honour to God every day if that is all you can do initially. If you already pray, take a step further and bring Him into your everyday life. If you struggle with prayer, start by praising Him and calling on His name. When you wake up in the morning, call upon His name and express gratitude for the breath you have received. And if you're already on fire for God and experience intimate prayer sessions, consider including Him in aspects of your life where you haven't invited Him before. Bring Him to work, invite Him into meetings, and make Him a constant presence.

In your church involvement, choose to partner with God if you are not involved with the service. I have personally entered into a partnership with God, where I work alongside Him to allow His Spirit to flow in the church whenever I am present. You can be in the background. You do not need to be on stage. Wherever you are in the church, you too can allow His Spirit to flow through you.

You can build yourself and connect with God on a deeper level in many ways. It does not have to be a one-way system. It does not have to be a singular way of communicating with God. You can play worship music daily in your house so that your whole household is filled with the Spirit of God. Be intentional about bringing God into your everyday life, wherever you are.

Where you would have filled your thoughts and your heart with different things, where the conversations in your home will be centred around worldly stuff and issues that would not bring any value to you, change it. Shift the focus towards talking and thinking about what God has done, is doing, and will do. Even if you feel that God hasn't done anything or you don't have anything to discuss, ask Him what He wants to do in your life and in the lives of those around you. Trust that He is always at work and has incredible plans in store.

By actively involving God in all aspects of your life, you will not only build a deeper connection with Him but also transform your mindset and surroundings to align with His will. Take the step today and commit to a life filled with God's presence and guidance.

> *Bless the Lord, O my soul, and all that is within me, bless His holy name. Bless the Lord, O my soul, and forget not all His benefits, who forgives all your iniquities, who heals all your diseases, who redeems your life from the pit, who crowns you with lovingkindness and tender mercies, who satisfies your mouth with good things, so that your youth is renewed like the eagle's.*
>
> **Psalm 103:1-5, MEV**

This brings us to reading the Bible, which can often be a challenge for many people. I completely understand and can relate to those who find it daunting. The Bible is a massive book, filled with different genres and countless chapters covering diverse stories and regulations. It can easily become confusing and overwhelming.

If you are new to reading the Bible, I recommend starting with the New Testament. Begin by reading the Book of John and encounter Jesus Christ Himself. You do not need to have the entire Bible memorised to feel connected to God. He can connect with you in various ways and forms.

Make a commitment to open your Bible every day, but do not let it become a mere habit or a task to tick off your list. Instead, approach Bible reading as your spiritual exercise with God. It is a way for you to encounter Him and express your love and gratitude. Each day, say to God, *"I love and thank you. What do you have for me today?"* Keep it simple and consistent by doing this every day.

Repetitive reading can be incredibly helpful. When a particular verse or passage is repeated to us, it holds deeper meaning. If you want to hear God directly speak to you through the Scriptures, pick one or two verses and read them repeatedly for a week. Ask Him what He is saying and pay attention to the words and phrases that stand out to you. You will find that these words and phrases will appear differently in your everyday life and interactions with others. That is God's way of capturing your attention and making His presence known in your life.

It is essential to understand that God did not call us to live in bondage, restricted by rules and regulations. Through Christ's sacrifice, He set us free and made us whole. We don't need to be bound by rules to encounter Him.

I can personally relate to living a life driven by the need to please others. Even when I wasn't feeling well, I would show up for church just so that people would see that I had been to church; *the man-pleasing spirit again.* But it doesn't have to be that way.

You go to church to commune with God and fellowship with other people. Sometimes circumstances may prevent you from physically attending; there is nothing wrong with that. God will be with you wherever you are. What you have to change in your mind is the understanding that whatever you are doing, Colossians 3:23 tells us to do everything as unto the Lord and not to man.

When you attend church on Sunday, it is important to remember that worshipping the Lord is your primary focus. While socialising with others is a valuable part of the church experience, if you are not also encountering God, it becomes nothing more than a regular gathering. The true essence of church is not simply attending a service, but it is about connecting with God both individually and as a community. You desire to meet God wherever you are, and you also desire others to experience His presence alongside you. Your heart longs for a genuine encounter with the living God. Therefore, it is crucial to break free from the mindset of being bound by rules and regulations. Instead, embrace the freedom Christ has won for you on the cross. Allow His liberating power to manifest in every aspect of your life, including your worship and interactions with others in the church community.

Remember, the purpose of going to church is to seek God's presence, to worship Him wholeheartedly, and to cultivate a transformative relationship with Him. As you walk in this freedom and authenticity, others will also be inspired to seek God in a genuine and life-changing way. Let your desire to meet God and lead others to Him be the driving force behind your church involvement.

Serving God involves various aspects of our lives. It includes how we handle our finances through giving, as well as practices like fasting that we will delve deeper into. However, the key is to allow the Spirit of God to guide our thoughts and actions.

When we yield to the leading of the Holy Spirit, we will begin to bear fruit that reflects God's character and aligns with His words. The abundant life that God offers is not characterised by bondage, limitations, fear, anxiety, insecurity, or doubt. On the contrary, God has set us free, made us righteous, and desires our wholeness.

As we surrender ourselves to the Spirit's influence, we will experience true freedom and discover a life filled with peace, joy, and security in God's love. It is through His power and grace that we are enabled to live a life that brings honour to Him and impacts others positively.

So, as you engage in various aspects of serving God, remember to rely on His Spirit for guidance. Allow His presence to influence your thoughts and actions. In doing so, you will bear fruit that is pleasing to Him and reflects His nature. Embrace the freedom that God has granted, and let Him transform every area of your life, making you whole and bringing glory to His name.

What you desire

One of the things that I really battled with was the desires placed inside me. I found myself drawn to things that other people were not interested in, and it left me feeling confused. It made me insecure because I couldn't understand why I had these desires and felt different. However, God revealed a profound truth to me: every desire within me is from Him because I carry His Spirit.

What that means for you is that you do not need to work up any passion for God. You do not need to work up any hunger or thirst for things of the spirit. God has placed His Spirit within you, which will influence the desires and passions you have. You may find yourself naturally waking up to pray at specific times or setting aside moments to read the Bible. These actions are not under your control; they are the result of God birthing those desires within you.

You may suddenly find yourself interested in something that is really not your *forte*. This is God's way of giving you an appetite and hunger for the things He wants you to pursue. You do not have to create these desires or manufacture feelings; they are already inside you, waiting to be discovered and expressed.

What God wants you to do, He would already have poured inside you, and it would just be you bringing it out. This truth is what Jesus had. He already knew the truth about His Father, so it was easy to translate it when He walked on the earth.

I discovered that all I wanted to do was not made up stuff, but He flowed out of me through ideas and desires. Let me ask you, *"What have you got? What has been throbbing in your heart? What can you not seem to dismiss, and if you shake it off, it keeps coming back?"* That is God tugging your heart. That is Him wanting to connect with you differently. And if you have not had any feelings like that, now is the opportunity to ask God, *"What exactly does He want you to focus on?"* You will witness Him shining light on various aspects of life for you.

We have all got something to contribute to this world. God is a creator, and He has placed desires and talents in every one of us. And you, my dear reader, have something extraordinary inside of you. You have got something that God specifically designed for you. It is time for you to partner with Him, birth it out, cause a change, and shift the environment around you.

Do not let everything that God has put into you lie dormant. He has served this food to you, and you cannot leave the food alone. You need to eat it. He has given you the appetite for it; now, you must work it out.

I can personally attest to this truth in my own life. Growing up, my mom was a writer, and I used to edit her stuff for her. I enjoyed reading over and making all the corrections here and there. And I loved reading and writing a little. But I did not know that God had put a gift of writing in me. I did not know that He had put creativity in me. Until I went through this journey with Him, and now I am writing and talking. What I was doing was not something I came up with. I didn't wake up one morning to become the person I am today. God had already created me for this purpose.

When God fashioned you, right down in your DNA was written who you are—the truth about yourself—and that is why you need Him. You need Him daily to reinforce and remind you of who you are, your worth, value, influence, and authority. This reality has deeply penetrated my husband and me, and we have embraced everything God offers. This truth resounded to us through our online school, Global Celebration School of Supernatural Ministry (GCSSM), which has become our lifeline. I was created an author before I ever got here. That is my truth. What is your truth?

So wherever you are, the fruits you bear will reflect the true nature of your soul and who you truly are. God is working within you to shape and reveal this. He desires for His children to walk in their authority, to resemble Him. There is much for you to accomplish on this earth, countless opportunities for you to influence.

When you cast your gaze upon the world, you will recognize the pervasive needs that surround us, some of which are uniquely assigned to you. Something out there is waiting for your impact, influence, change, and restoration. Somebody out there is waiting for your words of wisdom, your golden nuggets, to move forward with their life. If you are a parent, your children are awaiting your guidance to unlock their potential—it is already within you.

You are a remarkable individual. A good person. A good parent. A good spouse. You have been endowed with incredible gifts to offer to the world. Step out fearlessly. Conquer your giants. Tear down the walls of opposition. Allow God to flow through you, and you will see yourself doing stuff, facing challenges and climbing hills and valleys with a grace not attainable through your own efforts. This is what God desires to do with you.

Imagine the impact on a child when a parent recognizes their potential and worth, yet the child remains unaware. That is precisely what our Heavenly Father is communicating to us. He knows who you are. He knows what He has placed within you. He knows what you are capable of. He is saying, *"Go for it*, and I will be with you every step of the way."

There is a captivating account in the Bible about a man named Gideon who faced numerous challenges alongside his people. One day, he had an encounter with an angel that changed everything. The angel called him a *"mighty man of valour."* This proclamation bewildered Gideon because he saw himself as the least important in his family and his family the least in their kingdom. He felt like the nothingness of nothingness. And he received this proclamation as a mighty man of valour. Yet, as the story unfolds, Gideon transforms into a mighty warrior. He led his people against an overwhelmingly large and formidable army. God understood the dormant potential within Gideon, just as He understands what lies within you. God knows what He has placed inside you and how to bring it out; you work with Him. You engage with Him.

When you allow God to influence your thoughts and mind, He removes limitations and boundaries. He sets you free and makes you whole.

So, embrace the desires, talents, and passions that God has placed within you. Let them shine and impact the world around you. You are meant for greatness, and with God by your side, nothing is impossible.

Reel it in

You are enough for the season you are in. God created you with a perfect plan in mind for you to accomplish something on earth. In whatever sphere you are, you have been planted to make a difference, but you can only birth what is in you by aligning your thoughts and your truths with what the Father has for you. God has a plan, and it has got your name on it! Grab it and work with him into manifestation.

> *Not that we are fit (qualified and sufficient in ability) of ourselves to form personal judgments or to claim or count anything as coming from us, but our power and ability and sufficiency are from God.*
>
> **2 Corinthians 3:5, AMPC**

The Father desires to connect with you in all the diverse ways He has made available to you. There is no set or established method of communicating with Him. So be receptive and embrace God's many encounters with His children.

> *Each of you should use whatever gift you have received to serve others, as faithful stewards of God's grace in its various forms. If anyone speaks, they should do so as one who speaks the very words of God. If anyone serves, they should do so with the strength God provides, so that in all things God may be praised through Jesus Christ. To him be the glory and the power for ever and ever. Amen.*
>
> **1 Peter 4:10-11, NIV**

We are all created with different purposes and tasks, and we will master what God has given us if we engage with Him daily.

> *God has made us what we are. In Christ Jesus, God made us new people so that we would spend our lives doing the good things he had already planned for us to do.*
>
> **Ephesians 2:10, ERV**

Time of Reflection

► What is one thing you have found that has kept you limited?

► How does knowing that God created you in perfection change your view?

► God connects with us in diverse ways; which is your favourite, and which do you desire?

► Where is your greatest desire, and how can God align it with His will?

∞

Activation

Embark on an exciting journey with God and explore the various ways in which you can hear from Him. God purposefully gifted us with our five senses—sight, smell, hearing, taste, and touch—with the intention of communicating with us through each of them.

Take this opportunity to envision a life brimming with endless possibilities and let your imagination soar alongside God. Imagine Him generously offering you everything your heart desires, and then, inquire about His plans for you in the present moment.

Delight in your preferred approach to hearing from God while engaging all your senses to connect with Him. If you feel adventurous, you can try this with everything around you. Invite others to join you as you ask the Father to communicate with you through the objects around you.

∞∞∞

*Every single moment you are thinking
of me! How precious and wonderful to
consider that you cherish me constantly in
your every thought! O God, your desires
toward me are more than the grains of
sand on every shore! When I awake each
morning, you're still with me.*
Psalm 139:17-18, TPT

Five

I am Full

He gives me new strength. He guides me in the
right paths for the honor of his name.
Psalm 23:3, NIRV

There comes a significant moment in our lives when we are ready for the big jump. It may involve a major decision or a significant step forward. The Bible assures us that God does not give us anything beyond what we can handle, but He equips us with the capacity to receive everything He has planned for us.

If you've ever felt overwhelmed and out of your depth, I can empathize with you because I have experienced that too. That feeling of stagnancy and fear of tackling what is ahead can keep us bound and stagnant. So, how do we navigate these challenging situations?

When I joined my company, I was part of a trainee scheme that involved multiple placements in different areas of the company over two years. At the end of the program, there was an interview that everyone dreaded but also looked forward to because it meant moving on to the next stage. I went through that process, and I enjoyed it. My natural abilities in communication and presentation shone through, particularly in PowerPoint presentations. This was a gift from God, and I embraced it wholeheartedly.

After the interview, I had to decide on my next work area. Two options were presented to me. One seemed easier and more straightforward, the kind of choice that ordinary people would make to simplify their lives. Unfortunately, that was not my narrative.

Although I didn't want to choose the more challenging option, I felt a strong conviction that I should. I tried to shake it off, but it kept tugging at the back of my mind. I even tried praying against the perceived *"devil"* who wanted me to choose a difficult path destined for failure. However, no matter how hard I tried, I found peace only when considering that challenging option. It was clear that it was beyond my comfort zone, resembling a mountain waiting to be climbed. It was the one place that even people already experienced in my field avoided at all costs and had nothing positive to say about it.

Despite everything, I followed my intuition and chose that difficult path, firmly believing it was the direction I was meant to take. Interestingly, I did not have enough knowledge about this area to serve them how they needed to be supported. Since I was the first one out of the scheme, they entrusted it to me. I stepped into this role terrified and nervous, with no idea what I had gotten myself into.

It would be pleasant for me to say, " *Oh, everything went well. It was amazing. It was a beautiful experience."*

Unfortunately, it was not; life is more complex than that. It was hard. It was painful. This was a very complicated place, and it took people years to familiarise themselves with what was going on, as I was frequently reminded. I consistently found myself out of my depth, often unaware of what people were talking about. I was playing catch-up with everything that I was involved with.

For this reason, the confident me who was so fired up and did awesome stuff whilst on the trainee scheme and finished at the top of the class, ready to conquer the world, suddenly shrank in my depth and became the bottom of the class, grappling with feelings of inadequacy in this new setting. The confident conqueror turned into a beginner again.

Eyes on Him alone

It can get overwhelming when we are presented with many options, plans, and ideas. Instead of the many projects and ideas being a booster for us, they can often drown and bury us. The same goes for our path in life; we encounter many things, and if we do not know how to handle them, they can become overwhelming and create uncertainty. What God wants for you, if you find yourself burdened with a multitude of tasks, ideas, plans, and decisions, is to take it one step at a time. As the Lord orders your steps, He will guide you through whatever lies ahead of you.

> *The steps of a good man are ordered by the Lord, And He delights in his way.*
>
> **Psalm 37:23, NKJV**

Remember, life is not a race or a competition. You are here on your own journey. Your journey is tailored specifically for you. It does not have to resemble somebody else's. It does not have to look like what somebody else is doing. It should only look and feel like you. It should be entirely you.

It is crucial to know who you are in each season of life. This self-discovery is a gift that God has given to me. I had to examine everything happening around me and find myself at the core. It was like being submerged in a ball pit, surrounded by countless balls, unable to see myself clearly. However, God opened my eyes, and I could finally see. I could identify my strengths and the resources available to me. I focused on those aspects and devoted my energy to them.

We can draw inspiration from the story of Elisha and his servant Gehazi in 2 Kings 6. If you are familiar with the Prophet Elisha, you know that he provided prophetic guidance to the king of Israel during their war with the king of Aram. Whenever the Arameans conspired, Elisha revealed it to the king of Israel, much to the frustration of the king of Aram. This enraged the king of Aram, and he ordered that Elisha be captured. For this reason, the king of Aram sent his horses, chariots, and a strong force into the night, and they surrounded Dothan, where Elisha stayed. The king of Aram had not fully encountered the God of Israel and was ignorant of the move of His hand. So, to him, this was a done deal—Elisha was surrounded, and there was no escaping.

Rightly so, early the following day, when they woke up, Elisha's servant, Gehazi, saw this vast army, and he was immediately terrified and cried out to Elisha, his master. All around the city were these massive armies with their horses and chariots. Clearly, this was the end of Elisha, but to Gehazi's utter surprise, Elisha did not flinch. He was not perturbed at all. Then he said the most incredible thing.

"...Do not be afraid, for those who are with us are more than those who are with them."

2 Kings 6:16, AMP

Gehazi likely thought that Elisha must be losing it. However, Elisha prayed a prayer that changed everything for Gehazi: *"Open his eyes, Lord, so that he may see."* Oh, how we need this prayer in our daily lives! We need the Lord to fully open our eyes so we can clearly see as He sees. We should be like Elisha, unperturbed by the mountains that seek to devour us.

"Lord, open our eyes to see the reality of this world as you see it. Amen!" In this story, the Lord opened Gehazi's eyes, and he witnessed the hills full of horses and chariots of fire all around Elisha. Hallelujah! Amen! Yes, and Amen!

> *I pray that the Father of glory, the God of our Lord Jesus Christ, would impart to you the riches of the Spirit of wisdom and the Spirit of revelation to know him through your deepening intimacy with him. I pray that the light of God will illuminate the eyes of your imagination, flooding you with light, until you experience the full revelation of the hope of his calling —that is, the wealth of God's glorious inheritances that he finds in us, his holy ones!*
>
> **Ephesians 1:17-18, TPT**

Have you ever considered that when you feel completely alone and overwhelmed, the Lord might be revealing to you that He has a heavenly entourage surrounding you to guide and safeguard you?

God wants you to have this eye-opening experience from where you are in life. He desires for your eyes to be wide open so that you can see those who are with you. You can see exactly what He wants you to focus on. This way, when you have to make a choice, it is not unclear but rather evident and sharp. He wants to gift you with the ability to see into the future He has prepared for you.

Whenever you find yourself in a confusing place, ask God to open your eyes to see rightly, to see what He sees, and to hear what He hears. It changes everything.

There is a lot of noise in the world and around us, which can dampen our spirits. It can blind us to what God is doing. It can make us deaf to what God is saying. You must find a quiet place to say, *"God, show me. Show me what you see. Teach me what You want me to know."* Especially if you are in the middle of making important decisions, never jump in at any opportunity.

A wise man once said that if you must invest in something great or make a significant decision, do not rush into it. Give yourself at least 48 hours to think it through. If the decision you need to make cannot wait for 48 hours, that is your sign that you should walk away. Let it slide and go. I am not sure if this approach will work for your specific circumstances, but I constantly remind my husband about the need to deliberate before making significant decisions.

> But they that wait upon the LORD shall renew their strength; they shall mount up with wings as eagles; they shall run, and not be weary; and they shall walk, and not faint.
>
> Isaiah 40:31, KJV

The waiting season fills us with the strength and tenacity to soar higher when the time is right to make a choice. Allowing yourself to wait things out enables God to influence your decisions. The gift of the waiting period is that it will enable you to process your actions and contemplate your situation with God. You will see clearly when you spend time with God and discuss your choices. You are freed from fear and anxiety and you can hear His voice clearly. You become fully aware of God's will and direction for you.

May we continuously seek God's wisdom, open our eyes to His perspective, and find solace in waiting on Him. Through this, we will be empowered to make informed decisions and navigate our journey with confidence, knowing that He is guiding our every step.

A chunk at a time

The mesmerising thing I found about the new place they assigned me was that there was so much to be done, and I had somehow bought into the lie that I had to do it all. I had to make it all happen. I had to complete everything. That was a lie that held me bound. If you have ever found yourself in a place where it feels like you have a mountain ahead of you or that you need to complete anything, remember that you never have to do everything all at once.

Learning to tackle problems in small, manageable chunks was a game-changer for me. Knowing what can and cannot be done, where I need and do not need support, and understanding that timing is crucial. By organising my life and prioritising tasks, I prevented myself from constantly feeling overwhelmed. It is essential to recognise what you can handle at any given moment. Be kind to yourself, as my good girlfriend always reminds me.

Refuse to live in the fear that you are missing out on anything. Allow yourself to trust that things will fall into place with time. The fear of missing out often holds us back, causing us to act hastily. We often feel pressured to act, fearing that we will miss out on opportunities.

However, when we learn to be content with where we are and what we can do in the present, we realise that we don't need to rush. If something can wait, let it wait.

Sometimes, all it takes is the courage to ask for help. People are often more willing to assist than we realise. That was the blessing I discovered - people were ready and willing to guide me through processes and offer their support. So, never pressure yourself to do it all on your own. There is help and support around you.

> *So that we may boldly say, The Lord is my helper, and I will not fear what man shall do unto me.*
> **Hebrews 13:6, KJV**

Remember, you have your church community around you for a reason. I have discovered that having individuals who can encourage and guide me just by simply walking alongside me on this journey is invaluable.

Because sometimes the lie is that we are alone. We are the only ones facing this mountain. Only when you speak to others that you realise you are never alone. People are walking on the same journey as you, and you can all be there for each other. You can all be accountable to each other.

I have found the gifts of communities such a blessing. Being around like-minded people who will cheer you on, inspire you, and spur you on to the next goal God has for you is essential, so invest in them.

Refuse to struggle and travel alone. Make room in your life to let other voices in—positive voices. Do not be afraid to be vulnerable. It is acceptable to say, *"I cannot do this."* It is alright to say, *"I need help."* It is fine to be vulnerable because you know what? Someone within your circle has been where you are or going through what you are going through and it is only by opening up and asking for support that you will hear the rest of the story.

That was a precious life lesson for somebody who always thought I could get it all done. I learnt to say, *"I need help. I am ignorant, and I need support here."* I believe vulnerability is a gift God has given us so that we can make room for others to help. So that we can make room for Him to be our help, source and guide. He does not need you to struggle and try to make things happen.

> *So do not fear, for I am with you; do not be dismayed, for I am your God. I will strengthen you and help you; I will uphold you with my righteous right hand.*
>
> **Isaiah 41:10, NIV**

God told Adam and Eve that a man would leave his father and mother and be joined to his wife and become one. That is the reason He created marriage: companionship. In the same way, there is a reason why we have our church body—that we can do this together. Make use of the community that you have around you. Make them a part of your journey and be there for each other so you can be balanced in this life of fullness. You can have a well-balanced Christian life.

You must not live in isolation. Bring other people on board and share your journey with them. You will grow healthy mentally and emotionally if you do this. As you pour yourself into others, you will experience a richness in your own life and in the lives of those around you. The more you give, the more God fills you up, allowing you to do more.

The hills and valleys

As part of a charity event, my husband participated in the challenging task of climbing 24 peaks in 24 hours. It resembled a series of mountains with constant ups and downs, much like the journey of life itself. Hills and valleys, highs and lows, are inherent parts of life, and it is important to accept that as normal and natural.

When you find yourself on a mountain, embrace it and give it your all. Remember Nehemiah's words after the children of Israel had completed rebuilding their city wall,

> *Nehemiah said, " Go and enjoy choice food and sweet drinks, and send some to those who have nothing prepared. This day is holy to our Lord. Do not grieve, for the joy of the Lord is your strength."*
>
> **Nehemiah 8:10, NIV**

When God places you on your mountain in your new season, yes, give it your best effort.

Likewise, when you descend from the mountain and are down at the bottom pit in the valley, that is just part of life. Do not dwell too much on the negative aspects of your circumstances. Refrain from fixating on the fact that you are in a challenging season. Let it run its course and trust that it will eventually pass, regardless of its nature.

In my own experience, it looked like showing up for meetings and needing to be more knowledgeable about what was happening. When I did not know what was being discussed, I would often put a label on myself and put myself down unnecessarily. However, I came to realise that not knowing something is not a failure. Everyone experiences moments of learning and growth. I no longer needed to engage in self-loathing and negative self-labelling.

Being in a place of ignorance presents an opportunity to learn. It meant engaging with others and other resources to understand some processes. When you find yourself in a low season, allow it to unfold naturally. Soon enough, you will emerge from that place and discover ways to move forward.

There may be seasons where the pain might be so unbearable and it seems impossible to escape. You might find yourself lingering in such a place for an extended period. In these moments, it's essential to reset and reconnect with God.

> *The Lord himself goes before you and will be with you; he will never leave you nor forsake you. Do not be afraid; do not be discouraged."*
>
> **Deuteronomy 31:8, NIV**

If you are in a dreary place and cannot find your way out, this is the perfect time to ask God to help you. He will be by your side, just as He was with Job in moments of confusion and uncertainty. Trust that God is faithful and seeks to save and restore.

If you call on Him, He will rescue you out of the depths of your despair. God is swift to save, as Psalm 18 illustrates. Just as God delivered Jeremiah from the cistern, in chapter thirty-eight of the book of Jeremiah, He will pull you out of your own personal struggles.

Life is going to throw different things at you. You will find yourself in uncomfortable places as you strive for higher heights. These obstacles are all part of your journey. Understand that the highs and lows are all part of life and that each phase needs to run its course. Rest assured that you will not remain in one state forever. If you can keep your eye on God, you can allow life to be and accept that you cannot do it alone. You have the ability to overcome and rise above any circumstances you encounter.

Reel it in

God was very kind, generous, and gentle throughout my journey. Even when you find yourself in challenging circumstances and unfortunate places, He always comes through. This is a testament to His faithfulness and the nature of who He is. I experienced His help first-hand as He opened my eyes to what I was capable of and what I still needed to learn. I suddenly realised that I was in over my head. Not everything about that place was familiar to me. In fact, I did not need to know everything about it. That is simply the nature of my work and I needed to focus on honing my craft.

Initially, the magnitude of what was laid before me blinded my view. I could not see past the challenges, and it made me forget my own strengths and talents. Thankfully, God helped me recognise the gifts He had bestowed upon me. He taught me how to be patient with myself and the process of growth.

One important attribute God gifted me was humility, admitting to myself that I was inexperienced in my field and recognising the opportunity to learn from more experienced people.

So, instead of putting pressure on myself to perform and be like others, I humbly admitted, *"I do not know. I want to learn from you."* God granted me favour with people. No matter how long it took, I got the necessary answers when I asked the questions. I was no longer stuck in a place of defeat. I approached each step one thread at a time. The more I started unwinding the thread, the stronger I got, the wiser I got, and the more experienced I became. God created the opportunities for me to have more responsibilities.

Looking back, I no longer felt like the new person who joined the area. I have gained more experience and confidence, and sure of my abilities.

In one discussion with my line manager, after a few minutes of me sharing what I had been up to in my work area over the last quarter, she picked up on a vibe that blew her mind. Right before her was this transformed butterfly, no longer timid and intimidated by her job role. No longer seeking a way out. No longer gasping for breath. She let out this statement that literally got me giggling away in that meeting, which sounded like this: *"You are very confident now, Cathy. You are very happy now,"* to which I replied with all my excitement that I could not hold back: *"Yes, I am pleased because now I know what I can do. Now I have a nugget of what I am great at and that is what I am pursuing."* I had found my sense of purpose and direction. I was no longer lost.

Do not chase the wrong tree. Do not be too focused on getting things how you want them to be. Whatever is before you, take it one step at a time.

> *Within your heart you can make plans for your future, but*
> *the Lord chooses the steps you take to get there.*
> **Proverbs 16:9, TPT**

Allow God to build your skills, hone your skills, and show you precisely what you can do at any time. By focusing your energy on what He has placed before you, you can excel for His glory.

When you find yourself in the pit like Joseph did and cannot find any way out and you call His name, He will be right there. God, our great redeemer and helper, will be there with us. He has the power to restore all that seems lost.

Remember that this journey was never meant to be done alone. Surround yourself with people who will walk alongside you, and let God fill you up with His guidance and strength. Together, you can navigate through any challenges and achieve a fulfilling and balanced life.

Keep a cool head. Stay alert. The devil is poised to pounce, and would like nothing better than to catch you napping. Keep your guard up. You're not the only ones plunged into these hard times. It's the same with Christians all over the world. So keep a firm grip on the faith. The suffering won't last forever. It won't be long before this generous God who has great plans for us in Christ—eternal and glorious plans they are!—will have you put together and on your feet for good. He gets the last word; yes, he does.

1 Peter 5:8-11, MSG

You have a father who loves nothing more than showering your life with abundant resources. He has more than enough resources for you. He can restore what was lost and bring you into a place of abundance in His kingdom.

Instead of your shame you will receive a double portion, and instead of disgrace you will rejoice in your inheritance. And so you will inherit a double portion in your land, and everlasting joy will be yours.

Isaiah 61:7, NIV

Time of Reflection

- ► Do you struggle to let go of the reins?
- ► Do the people in your life influence you positively?
- ► Are you willing to lift your hand and ask for help?
- ► God is your ultimate helper; can you partner with Him in your assignment?

∞

Activation

Spend time to deeply reflect on all the plans and desires God is calling you to pursue. Write them all down, creating a comprehensive list. Then ask God these questions about each of them. *Where does this fit into my life? What am I supposed to do with them? Who am I supposed to connect with?* As you engage in this process, you will realise all these overwhelming ideas and plans will have their place and time in your life, and you can approach them one step at a time. Trust in God's wisdom and know that He will provide the direction and resources needed for each step of the journey.

∞∞∞

*Thank you for making me so wonderfully
complex! It is amazing to think about.
Your workmanship is marvelous—
and how well I know it.*
Psalm 139:14, TLB

Six

In the Overflow

You pour oil of blessing on my head;
you fill my cup to overflowing.
Psalm 23:5b, NCV

Currently, I am a part of a dedicated group that meets regularly, primarily to encourage and motivate one another and act as a beautiful support system for one another. Over the years, we have discovered that getting everyone online to join the meeting is a significant hassle. Most of us are worn out and would rather sleep than join. It has been fascinating to witness how the dynamics of our sessions have evolved.

Initially, when attending the meetings, we would often assume that we were the only ones who had endured a taxing day and craved an early night. To our surprise, we discovered that everyone in the group shared a similar sentiment. Despite this weariness, once the meeting commenced, something remarkable would occur. God would step in and transform the atmosphere, resulting in a completely different experience. However, this was not always the case.

It all started that year—the year we will remember for a long time. Yes, I am referring to the year that the world stood still. My friends and I had been conversing about how we could support each other by getting together and praying regularly. Well, it was just an idea, and we had bounced it off each other a few times.

Then the COVID-19 pandemic happened, and we decided that was the time to kick things off. I felt really strongly about it. There was so much chaos and uncertainty in our world, and we felt God wanted us to bring some stillness and peace to our circles. Therefore, we reached out to a few people, and many were hungry for spiritual upliftment. We just needed a place to get together regularly, pray about the issues at hand, and cover each other in prayer. And that is exactly what we did.

> *The Spirit of the Sovereign Lord is on me because the Lord has anointed me to proclaim good news to the poor. He has sent me to bind up the broken-hearted, to proclaim freedom for the captives and release from darkness for the prisoners, to proclaim the year of the Lord's favour and the day of vengeance of our God, to comfort all who mourn.*
>
> **Isaiah 61:1-2, NIV**

We felt connected to that passage and we believed God was calling us to embody its message. That is how our group was birthed—we became known as Isaiah 61. People from different parts of the world joined us, and together, we experienced the joy of doing life together.

As with everything else, we had to navigate troubled waters while keeping everyone afloat. We managed these by supporting each other and praying and covering everyone. As COVID-19 restrictions eased off, we even attempted some face-to-face meetings with those who were local to us, while others joined online. We could gather in various locations, fellowship, pray, and then meet online with our members, who still had to join in from outside the UK.

Over time, we sensed God calling us into a deeper relationship with him. We recognised it was time to deepen our roots in the word of God and not solely focus on prayer. This led us to identify ourselves with the Gatekeepers mentioned in 1 Chronicles 9:22-27. The Gatekeepers had the prime role of protecting and covering the people around them; that is what we became. This became our new vision. As a consequence, our group grew smaller, as not everyone desired to be part of this new direction. Building each other deep in the word of God, sharpening our spiritual senses, and just being a source of refreshing waters was what Gatekeepers became about. Personally, I found it to be a place of peace. Within the group, I had the privilege of seeing my friends, sisters, brothers, and even my younger sister.

We have been a part of each other's lives since then and continue to be. We have seen the ups and downs we have all had to go through and what it feels like to have a community around you. I found myself changing a lot over the years. Transforming my perspective from poverty to royalty, recognising myself as the royal being that God made me to be. He called me to lead the group and kept us united.

As I said, it has been amazing. Still, it has also been challenging, leading people, motivating and encouraging us, and getting us to get together. A few times, this has felt like a climb, and we have asked if we should keep going. However, each time we felt unable to press on, God intervened, providing strength and enabling us to continue. He has taught us to make necessary changes when things didn't seem to be working correctly.

The thing about pruning

Are you feeling stuck in the middle of a challenging climb? Often, we embark on good endeavours, knowing they are valuable and necessary, but we underestimate the difficulties they may bring. We expect things to be easy because they are good, right? However, it can be frustrating when it feels like events are simply happening without aligning with our desires. We long to make an impact, overcome obstacles, and be influential.

Reflecting on the journey of our group—where we started from, the hurdles we had to face, and where we are currently, I know that I saw God prune me personally. The person that I was a few years ago underwent a profound transformation. Each day, when I felt overwhelmed and at my breaking point, God removed things from my life, broke bad habits, and shifted my circumstances. He revealed weaknesses in me, prompting me to confront the reality of who I truly was and be willing to change.

So, if you find yourself in a season where you feel like, *"God, this should be easier,"* but it is not, it is because God is pruning you. God is taking away the things you consider desirable and appropriate for your current situation because He knows they are not beneficial. This process may come in all forms: people, conditions, and your attitude. Personally, I encountered a lot of challenges with my attitude, and God helped me confront them and remove them from my life.

I am the true vine, and my Father is the gardener. He cuts off every branch in me that bears no fruit, while every branch that does bear fruit he prunes so that it will be even more fruitful.

John 15:1-2, NIV

One of the ways God accomplishes this is to pull us out of the crowd, out of the noise and chaos, and He invites us to spend intimate time with Him. It could come as an intimate day, as one of my friends calls it. She set up a regular monthly intimate day with God, where she shuts out her world. She is swamped, but once in a while, she shuts out her world and spends the whole day with God, seeking His face.

For me, it often takes the form of fasting. Fasting says to God, *"I'm laying my tummy down for you."* Whether you enjoy fasting or do not have any relationship with fasting at all, I found fasting a way to surrender myself to God. I lay myself down and say no to that chocolate my soul craves or that simple, healthy fruit that could give me good nutritional value. If you have ever fasted, you know this is what it looks like. You can go through the whole day without eating anything, and you will not be hungry, but as soon as you choose to fast, the hunger pangs come alive in your tummy. Everything smells and tastes good and looks so delicious. To overcome that and conquer it, I feast on the Spirit of God through prayer and His word. God strengthens me and I find my fulfilment in Him.

Consider setting aside a day, even if it's just a half-day; if you find yourself in a situation where you feel that things are difficult, you cannot see a way out and you are confronting challenges. Decide to have your own intimate day with God, beginning with just putting that phone away. Put that phone away and resolve to spend an intimate day with God. Shut out everything in your life and spend time with Him.

I have had fasting days when I am busy at work, which still works. I do not need to stop my life so I can fast. It is all about my heart posture and where I direct my Spirit. So, if I am working and fasting, I focus on God the whole day. I will be in meetings, sitting in my office, and allowing His words to flow through me.

> *Then, when you fast, don't look like those miserable play-actors! For they deliberately disfigure their faces so that people may see that they are fasting. Believe me, they have had all their reward. No, when you fast, brush your hair and wash your face so that nobody knows that you are fasting—let it be a secret between you and your Father. And your Father who knows all secrets will reward you.*
>
> **Matthew 6:16-18, PHILLIPS**

Fasting is a way God uses to clear the clutter out of our lives, because the only way you can make space for the new is by getting rid of the old stuff in your life that has made you comfortable and secure.

Create space in your life for God to fill you, for God to enter and carry out all the old things that are happening there so that you can begin to resemble precisely how He wants your life to look.

Abundance mindset

Embracing the blessings God has in store for you can be overwhelming as you reflect on your past and present experiences. Gatekeepers gave me the community and support I had longed for. In the past, the enemy bombarded me with negative thoughts, causing me to feel abandoned, rejected, and like a failure. However, through Gatekeepers, I found a community that became like family—friends and sisters who are always there for me. But it took a total mindset shift to see myself as the new creation I had become—a royal priesthood, a holy nation, and a chosen generation. I believe that God desires the same transformation for you.

> *God can do anything, you know—far more than you could ever imagine or guess or request in your wildest dreams! He does it not by pushing us around but by working within us, his Spirit deeply and gently within us. Glory to God in the church! Glory to God in the Messiah, in Jesus! Glory down all the generations! Glory through all millennia! Oh, yes!*
>
> **Ephesians 3:20-21, MSG**

God wants you to be an influencer wherever you are, and this is possible when you adopt an abundance mindset and recognise your authority. You can speak like Jesus spoke. Jesus never doubted the Spirit moving through Him; He simply spoke to the situations, and they aligned with His words. That was what the apostles did, and that is what God wants us to do. He wants us to speak to situations and command them to align with His will and purpose. When you live, talk, and think like the royal individual that you are, you will have a positive influence on your environment.

In the Bible, a man named Jabez underwent a mindset shift that transformed his life (1 Chronicles 4:9-11). The Bible says he was named Jabez because his mother gave him birth in pain. For a long time, pain and misery were all he knew. It filled his life with gloom and frustration. Until one day, he decided he was tired of that life and prayed a prayer out of his comfort zone.

> *"...Oh, that You would bless me indeed, and enlarge my territory, that Your hand would be with me, and that You would keep me from evil, that I may not cause pain!..."*
>
> **1 Chronicles 4:10, NKJV**

The Bible says God heard his prayer. At that moment, Jabez's life was completely turned around, and he walked in abundance.

God wants you to influence systems and walk in authority. He wants you to operate in the environment where you are, and you can do that when you partner with Him. When you take hold of His truth, His truth that says that you are the head and not the tail, His truth that says that you can do all things through Him that strengthens you, His truth says that you can pull down this mountain. God wants the truth that He speaks to you to resonate deep in your spirit so that you can walk and talk like the royal person you are and exercise the authority He has given you.

> *But you belong to God, my dear children. You have already won a victory over those people, because the Spirit who lives in you is greater than the Spirit who lives in the world.*
> **1 John 4:4, NLT**

In the Gatekeepers community, many of us faced challenges. However, whenever we got together, we spoke life over each other. In our small group, we have witnessed miracles in each other's lives. We have seen our authority in Christ grow, commanding sicknesses to leave and causing things to shift in people's families. We have seen that happen in our group, and I believe God wants the same thing for you. He wants you to partner with Him, declare His words, and trust in His plans for your life. While you may feel full and filled up where you are right now, God has much more for you and wants you to have an abundance mindset. God can do much more than you ask or think.

> *Then the Lord your God will prosper you abundantly in every work of your hand, in the children of your womb, the offspring of your cattle, and in the produce of your ground, for the Lord will again rejoice over you for good, just as He rejoiced over your fathers, if you obey the LORD your God, to keep His commandments and His statutes which are written in this Book of the Law, if you turn to the LORD your God with all your heart and soul.*
> **Deuteronomy 30:9-11, NASB**

The surrendered heart

To be able to fulfil your calling as an influencer, you must surrender to God's authority. Jesus Himself taught His disciples that the person who wants to lead must first learn to serve. In the Kingdom of God, being a leader means embracing a different model—one of servanthood and humility.

> *Jesus, knowing their thoughts, called them to his side and said, "Kings and those with great authority in this world rule oppressively over their subjects, like tyrants. But this is not your calling. You will lead by a completely different model. The greatest one among you will live as the one who is called to serve others, because the greatest honor and authority is reserved for the one with the heart of a servant. For even the Son of Man did not come expecting to be served but to serve and give his life in exchange for the salvation of many."*
>
> **Matthew 20:25-28, TPT**

Gatekeepers community has provided us with the opportunity to embody this servant leadership. We founded the group together, and although we are seen as its leaders, we are also part of it. We are there to serve each other, to support each other, to strengthen each other, and to be in each other's lives. Our role is to make room for others to flourish, and every leader must learn to lay down their tools and craft and allow others the space to grow and develop.

I have found it such a delight and a joy to see the members of Gatekeepers walking in their stride and doing amazing things in the kingdom on their Christian journey. I am privileged to be a part of that, but that only happened because we chose to surrender. We decided to lay it all at His feet. We gave God the ideas we were processing so He could have His way.

God blesses you abundantly when you decide not to withhold from others but give out to others. The Bible said in Luke 6:38,

> *"Give generously and generous gifts will be given back to you, shaken down to make room for more. Abundant gifts will pour out upon you with such an overflowing measure that it will run over the top! The measurement of your generosity becomes the measurement of your return."*

If you are not a giver and struggle to give money, a wise man said, *"Make God your money manager."* Recognise that everything that you have is from Him. There was a time when we were struggling with Gatekeepers, and it was getting hard because people were all busy. But God taught me a valuable lesson, and I think that is what has held us together. He showed everyone, especially me, that the group belonged to Him. While I have my name on it, it is not mine; God is the actual leader. Each member of the group, including myself, was His child, doing something together that we may not fully comprehend. So, I learnt to lay Gatekeepers at His feet, for Him to have His way, to move how He wants, and to direct as He wants to lead. So, if we had the meeting and we had an agenda and, the Spirit led us in a different direction than our agenda, we would not stand in the way; we would yield and allow His Spirit to flow.

We have witnessed the incredible impact when we allow the Spirit of God to do what He wants to do and not stand in His way because we have an agenda. We learned to throw our agendas away and allow God's agenda to be the primary guide and leader in everything we do.

I encourage you to start giving generously, even with the little that you have. Sow into ministries, support those in need, and be a blessing wherever you can. You will discover that God will fill you up when you give out what you have. I know what that looks like. Since we gave our finances to God, we have never had a time of need. We keep providing for various needs and responsibilities, and we look at everything and ask, *"How are we managing this?"* We do not even know. But we know we are doing things and God is taking care of us in His own way.

We have been immensely blessed by a program called Wealth With God by Jim Baker. His teaching revolutionised our lives and taught us what it means to walk financially in the Kingdom of God, and his favourite saying that has caught on with us is: *"Nobody can take better care of me than Dad."* We found that nobody can take better care of us than God because He has better thoughts, all His thoughts are for our good, and He is always seeking our best interests.

Reel it in!

In the early stages of our group, we did not know that in a few years, we would look back on our lives and realise how every one of us had grown so much in our walk with God. We have been captivated by the things of the Spirit because we have seen the impact on our lives.

Keep going because God is with you and He is pruning and making everything right, like the porter moulds and builds. You will only see how far you have come and how amazing you look when you look back on the journey that you have been on with God.

No discipline seems pleasant at the time, but painful. Later on, however, it produces a harvest of righteousness and peace for those who have been trained by it.
Hebrews 12:11, NIV

When God is pruning, it is not pleasant, but when you endure it, when you endure the humility and patience, you will see the fruit. You will see your relationships getting better. You will know how to relate to people. You will know how to walk in the kingdom. You will know how to be the person God created you to be. I have learnt to surrender my life to God fully to bear the fruit I want to see.

You have a God who is always working on your behalf. That is what God does. He is working behind the scenes. He is moving and making things happen on your behalf. When you wake up every day, He is already ahead of you and planned out your whole day for you. That is what Psalm 139 says: *"Before I'd ever seen the light of day, the number of days you planned for me were already recorded in your book."* That is what God does.

You do not have to worry. You get to trust in God and lay everything at His feet. No matter what is going on or your life's current state, if you feel like it is not progressing as you want, know that God is at work. It is always going to be a work in progress. We will not reach the end of this journey with God as long as we breathe. We do not reach a point when we have got it all sorted. We have got it all covered. We know what we are doing. We are content. We are satisfied. No, we do not have that luxury. He gets to do that for us because He is Omnipotent. He is all-mighty. He has got all the authority. His powers and knowledge of our lives are too great for us to comprehend. We have a limited mindset about our lives. So, it is about walking with Him and letting Him reign.

When you are totally surrendered to God and give Him every aspect of your life, you do not get to keep any part of it out of His sight. You give every aspect of your life back to Him. What happens is that when you give it all to Him, He fills you, and you overflow, and it goes back to Him, and it becomes a cycle of blessings. God needs nothing from you. He wants to bless you but can only pour into you when you have given Him access to your heart. Empty yourself so that God can fill you up. God has so much that He does not fill the cup to complete it. He pours into you so that you will overflow. So, if you want to see yourself flowing in the Spirit, moving in His power, moving in His authority, then lay down any part of your life you feel entitled to, anything in your life that you feel strongly about.

God told Abraham he would have descendants as numerous as the stars in the sky. That did not make sense because He did not even have a child. But then God gave him the one, and one day, when he was enjoying his son, God told him to give him back. What would you have done when you had nothing and God gave you something and one day, He comes up and says, *"Give me the one thing that I gave you?"* I would not be willing and generous enough to return it to Him because I wanted it so badly. But we know the story of Abraham. We are the descendants of Abraham. When Abraham let go of his only son and was about to stab him, God stopped him and out of that trust, everyone else was born. Abraham had learnt to trust in his God. He understood what it means to let go, release and let God take over.

God is asking you to give every aspect of your life to him. Let him take over and be the final voice concerning anything in your life. For every decision you must make, let him be the one you discuss with.

In my own life, I have often found myself going back to God and asking Him questions before I even open my mouth and talk to anyone else. When I opened up to Him, He filled me with Him and replenished me to overflowing.

Now, in Gatekeepers, when we get together, we are a lifeline for each other. We are there for each other. We are growing together. We encourage each other. It is like the natural stream of living waters, a place where each one of us, every time we get together, never leaves empty. Every time we get together, the Father comes and pours back into us to overflow. We are excited to see where God will lead us next, for He has a divine plan for our community.

Time of Reflection

- ▶ Do you enjoy holding on to stuff?
- ▶ Are you willing to let God move things away from your life to make room for the new?
- ▶ Do you find excuses for the good God is bringing you?
- ▶ Which areas of your life have you kept away from God?
- ▶ God is constantly working on you; can you be pliable clay and let Him mould you into His perfect masterpiece?

∞

Activation

I will present you with three challenges, and I invite you to choose the one that resonates most with your current feelings.

Challenge 1: Embracing God's Pruning

If you have ever felt that things should be easy or smooth but instead find yourself facing challenges, it could be a sign that God is pruning you. He is pulling the dead and unnecessary aspects of your life to make you better in the field where he has placed you. Present everything to Him and have an open conversation with your Heavenly Father. Trust that He is working for your growth and refinement.

Challenge 2: Overcoming Past Experiences

If you find that your past experiences are still clouding your current state and you are still struggling to embrace all the goodness and blessings God is giving you, it is time to give your mind to God so you can have the mind of Christ. The mind of Christ walked in authority, power, and dominion. One way you can do this is by asking yourself these questions: *What is the one thing you know only God could make happen in your life?* Reflect on and remember the moments when He has shown His power and faithfulness. Let these encouragements empower you to face any mountains that may come your way.

Challenge 3: Surrendering All to God

You may be having a difficult time surrendering. After all, you have easily given Him parts of your life, but hold on to other aspects because you do not believe anyone can help you. But it is that very thing God is coming after because He is the all-in kind of God. He does not ask for part of our lives; He asks for all of them. So, I want to ask you: *What is one thing you are holding on to or struggling to let God handle for you?* Identify the things you are struggling to hand over to God and list them out. Take each item and genuinely hand it back to Him, symbolically laying it before Him. Once you have handed them all back to God, you take them and rip them apart until all you have left are just pieces of paper and your heart free, ready to embrace this new life of abundance, a royal mindset, total surrender of every aspect of life to God, no longer holding anything back, but a life where you allow God to move and flow through you, so He can spill out into all areas of your life.

∞∞∞

Is there anyplace I can go to avoid your
Spirit? to be out of your sight? If I climb to
the sky, you're there! If I go underground,
you're there! If I flew on morning's wings
to the far western horizon, You'd find
me in a minute— you're already there
waiting! Then I said to myself, "Oh, he
even sees me in the dark! At night I'm
immersed in the light!" It's a fact: darkness
isn't dark to you; night and day, darkness
and light, they're all the same to you.
Psalm 139:7-12, MSG

Seven

All are Welcome

*Certainly, your faithful protection and
loving provision will pursue me where I
go, always, everywhere. I will always be
with the Eternal, in Your house forever.*
Psalm 23:6, VOICE

y friend, congratulations on reaching the final chapter of
this book. Thank you for going on this adventure with
me. Thank you for entrusting me with your personal
space and I honour you for believing that God wants you to live this
life of intimacy with Him. God wants to be a part of your everyday,
everywhere, and every time lifestyle, where He becomes the defining
moment in everything you do. I appreciate you being here for the
conclusion of this book.

In many Christian communities, there are common questions
that weigh us down and hinder our progress. *"What is my ministry?"*

is one of such questions. This is a common inquiry among those who have been involved in the church for some time as they seek to discern their area of service.

Perhaps you also have questions about where you want to serve, where you want to sow your seeds and the organisations you want to support. You may wonder, *"Where is the place I can put my effort?"*

It can be disheartening when individuals with valuable contributions feel like their offerings are not wanted, similar to how David, the shepherd boy, was not readily accepted by King Saul despite his victory over Goliath. Have you ever found yourself asking, *"Why do I have so much to offer, but it seems like nobody wants it?"*

In moments of frustration with the system and circumstances around us, we may even contemplate going out on our own. If you have ever found yourself thinking, *"Can I do this independently?"* know that you are not alone.

If any of these questions resonate with you, I want to affirm your resilience in seeking answers. I believe that God has a purpose and a place for you. God has freely and generously equipped you with all His gifts and He wants you to pour them into fertile soil so that you will bear fruit.

Allow me to share a personal experience from our marriage. For the first time in our marriage, you will be surprised to learn that we had the privilege of having someone look after our children during a very hectic time so we could attend an international conference. We had just moved to a new home and booked this conference. One of our friends (God bless her heart) took on our three children and looked after them so we could go away and be a part of this conference.

As a result, the two of us sat by ourselves for the first time alone at the airport, on the plane, in our hotel room and this new city, reminiscing and discussing how we got here.

Finally, we made it to the conference centre. This was a global evangelical conference with hundreds of speakers lined up to deliver God's golden nuggets. Several workshops were running concurrently. There was a lot to give and a lot to pour. I did not know what to expect. A lot had been poured into this conference and we were privileged to be a part of it all.

Then God gave us a special gift in somebody from GCSSM and he became an incredible support system because he lived in Holland and made the entire experience extra special.

So why do I share this with you? Amsterdam 2023 was accessible to everyone; something awaited you regardless of your background, where you were headed, or what you had to offer. For the first time, I was in an environment that said, *"Whatever you are, whoever you are, wherever you are, just come on board, and you will feel right at home."* The first few days could simply be described as wild and heavenly.

Then, on the final day, they organised for us to go into the city to share Christ with everyone we met. It was both a thrilling and nerve-racking moment for me. I was being pushed out to do something I had always wanted; I was desperate and terrified to do it. Gathering with others, we were divided into groups to cover multiple parts of the city, go out and be what Jesus asked us to be—His hands and feet—and bring the good news to Amsterdam.

Ministry is a lifestyle

The whole worry and anxiety weighing me down about our ministry were debunked from my life. I realised that our ministry is not a building. Our ministry is not a place where you go and do something. Our ministry is the person of Jesus Christ living in and flowing out of us and that does not relegate us to the confines of a single space or institution. As long as you wake up every morning and you have a breath, you have an opportunity to minister to others. Your whole life becomes a ministry.

So, if for your whole life, you have been asking, *"Where is my ministry?"* You are the ministry. Your life is the ministry.

The Bible encourages us that the first place you minister is the very place that you wake up to and the people that you wake up around (1 Timothy 3).

If you are single, your ministry is where you live and the very people you interact with are your first ministry. They are the people who want to see the impact of Jesus in your life. They are the people you want to wake up to and ask God, *"How can I be a blessing to them?"*

If you are a family person, married, or have children, your inner nuclear institutes are your most important ministry. They are the first people you want to put everything you received from your Father into. The people you pour into, in whatever way, should be your priority when considering how to serve the Father.

Whatever state of life you are in, your whole life is a ministry. God has designed explicitly that wherever you are, once you open yourself, He will flow right out of you. You will spill out of wherever you are, and He will make you a blessing as you allow Him to flow out of you into your environs.

So, whether you are in the grocery store, whether you are at the play park with your children, whether you are at a work cafeteria or in a board meeting, wherever you find yourself, opportunities are presented to you to bring the glory of God that resides inside of you out there. Make it your mission to let Christ's Spirit flow out of you.

You do not need a megaphone to shout at your work and say, *"Come to Jesus."* You do not need to do all that. There is a time and space for that. We have a time and place to evangelise as a group. But in your personal walk with God, your life speaks the loudest to the people around you.

Make it your life mission to impart God into your circles. You will be surprised at how many people will be impacted by just watching how you live your life. You may never hear what people have to say. People see when there is glory in a person, but they might not have the vocabulary for it, and sometimes it might sound like this: *"There is just something about you!"* So be intentional about pouring out and letting Christ be known in you. Paul says in Colossians 4:6 to let your speech be seasoned so that you may know how to answer everyone. That is your primary ministry. Everything else will fall into place as you faithfully live out your call to be a vessel of God's love and light.

> *Friends, this world is not your home, so don't make yourselves cozy in it. Don't indulge your ego at the expense of your soul. Live an exemplary life in your neighborhood so that your actions will refute their prejudices. Then they'll be won over to God's side and be there to join in the celebration when he arrives.*
>
> **1 Peter 2:11-12, MSG**

The resource manager

As you start pouring yourself into various places, you will realise that God will open up heavenly sources and pour them into you. He will guide you to the places where he wants you to make an impact.

If you are wondering how and where you should sow or where you should support, remember that He gave what you have got to you, knows why He gave it to you and knows where He wants you to impact. So, speak to God about whatever you have got in your hand. It is not a matter of simply assessing the situation and deciding to jump in.

The Bible recounts a time when the prophet—the only prophet at that time—had the ear of God. He got it muddled up himself when he went to anoint the next king after King Saul. He went to a house, and being human like you and I are, he assumed that because people looked a certain way, they were the best fit for what he needed. But God taught him the lesson of life.

We are limited in our knowledge and insight into any situation; for that reason, we will always need God to be in the when and how of our thought processing and in all our decision-making. By connecting with the Spirit of God, Prophet Samuel was able to locate the right son from Jessie's home to anoint to be the next king.

> But the Lord said to Samuel, "Don't judge by a man's face or height, for this is not the one. I don't make decisions the way you do! Men judge by outward appearance, but I look at a man's thoughts and intentions."
>
> **1 Samuel 16:7, TLB**

God will lead you to the places where He wants you to serve. Do not be surprised if you have your sights set on a position or area of service that you believe is the ideal fit for you and think it fulfils all your needs, only for God to take you somewhere else. I apologise if this disappoints you, but it is important to understand that God wants you to surrender what's in your hands and let Him guide you to where you're needed.

You may not get the obvious choice. It may look different from what you think it should. It might turn out differently because the Omniscient God sees all things. He knows when and where needs are, what support is required, and what you are equipped to serve and bring an answer to. If you want to do it for His glory, then let Him be the one who will lead you to the space, to that area, and to the person to support you.

> *There are different kinds of gifts. But they are all given to believers by the same spirit. There are different ways to serve. But they all come from the same Lord. There are different ways the spirit works. But the same God is working in all these ways and in all people. The Holy Spirit is given to each of us in a special way. That is for the good of all. To some people the spirit gives a message of wisdom. To others the same spirit gives a message of knowledge. To others the same spirit gives faith. To others that one spirit gives gifts of healing. To others he gives the power to do miracles. To others he gives the ability to prophesy. To others he gives the ability to tell the spirits apart. To others he gives the ability to speak in different kinds of languages they had not known before. And to still others he gives the ability to explain what was said in those languages. All the gifts are produced by one and the same spirit. He gives gifts to each person, just as he decides.*
>
> **1 Corinthians 12:4-11, NIRV**

At first, it may be difficult to relinquish control and let God dictate where you should serve, but you realise that when God tells you to follow that voice and you do what He asks you to do, you will be blessed. You will be fulfilled; you will be enriched. You realise that everything you have in you that you want to pour is perfect for the area you need to flow into.

Allow God to be the manager of your resources, directing you to where support is needed. It is like in the UK, where we have the Jobs Centre; they mainly guide struggling people to find a job based on their skill set and available vacancies. Often, they are very successful at finding a suitable place of work. Like resource managers, they understand your capabilities and can connect you to the right opportunities. That is precisely what the Spirit of God wants to do for you. Anyone who has gone through such a process knows that it is easier to find a job when guided by a resource manager than when you rely solely on your own efforts.

Will you allow God, the ultimate resource manager, to match you with the perfect places? He wants to be your matchmaker. He wants to bring what He has poured into you directly to where He wants you to pour it so that you can experience fulfilment and enrichment through obedience. Trust Him and follow His leading.

Outside the boat

Have you ever felt frustrated and dissatisfied with your environment because you were not allowed to serve in the capacity you believed you deserved? I understand that feeling all too well. I have been in spaces where I have thought, *"I can do that. I want to do that."* But let me tell you, as God has shown me, what He has for you is not limited to the confines of any specific space. Do you know why? Because they are real people waiting and seeking love and care wherever you are.

You cannot spend your life discontented with a leader because they used their discretion to decide what they wanted their ministry to look like. They have made a choice about the place God has assigned them, and you also need to discern the place where God wants you to pour out your gifts and abilities.

The church plays a minimal role in your entire lifetime as a child of God. After a couple of hours on a Sunday, the church is over and then you spend the rest of your life outside the church. So, does that mean your ministry ends there? Would it not make sense for God to assign you a place where you spend the most significant portion of your life?

Outside the church, the entire world is your oyster. Can you imagine? Everywhere you turn, some people are hungry and thirsty, desperate for what is inside of you and you get to actually pour what God has given you into them.

This is where you get to use all the gifts that He has given you. So, whether you have the gift of wisdom, knowledge, faith, healing, power to do miracles, ability to prophecy, discernment of spirits, speaking in different languages, or interpreting different languages, there is something for you!

You must bring all these gifts that God has generously given you to life in the world around you. You connect with others and serve your local community. It begins with being intentional about being present for your neighbours. You will become a source of blessings for others if you start by being intentional with people, praying for them, and asking God for the things they need and desire to have in their lives. God has entrusted you with all His gifts, blessings and heavenly resources so you can bring them everywhere you go.

> *He said to them, "Go into all the world. Preach the good news to everyone."*
>
> **Mark 16:15, NIRV**

Jesus expects that wherever you are, you will witness about Him. So, I want to challenge you to be comfortable stepping outside the boat if you have ever wondered about ministering as Jesus commanded. Yes, you can!

There are people that God will connect you with to do this together. Be ready with a willing heart to say, *"Lord, use me wherever I am."*

God will bring other people with you who you can do this with. And once you realise that each time you choose to leave the safety of the boat and bring Jesus into where you are, He will manifest Himself, so long as you are willing to let the Spirit of God flow in and out of you. Oh yes! I have tested it, and it worked.

Reel it in!

In Amsterdam, we were sent out in groups of three into the streets of Amsterdam, and one after the other, we met people. Some were busy with their lives and walked away after giving us a quick hello. Others opened up their hearts and invited us to chat with them. With no preparation and no planning, we opened our mouths. We saw walls breaking down. Some people surrendered. We met some needs in that short time. We brought somebody home to the fold of Christ, and he received his deliverance and healing from an injury. All this happened on that day in Amsterdam.

So, are you ready? Are you ready to go out there and be everything God has called you to be? Are you ready to wake up every time and let Christ be the centre of everything happening around you? Are you ready to bring God on board wherever you go and wherever you are? Are you ready to feast on what God has served before you? Are you ready for God to influence you and give you the authority to take dominion in the spaces you are in? Are you ready for God to lead you into the exact places that require your pour and that He needs you to pour into?

Every fibre of you responds to the Spirit of God and is ready to be used by God. So, congratulations on rediscovering your true self. See how far you have come. God is expressing Himself fully through you, and it will also show up in time.

Allow God to lead you to where you can serve and support the people in your life. Never, ever be afraid to step outside the boat. Peter defied the odds and had the audacity to ask Jesus to let him come out of the boat and into the waters, and he did. He did something none of the other disciples ever got to do.

The ball is in your court; the red carpet has been rolled. Walk confidently! Walk in your intimacy with your Father, in your everyday, everywhere, every time lifestyle, as the Father leads and guides you.

Time of Reflection

- ► Where is the one thing God is calling you to?
- ► Are you ready for God to lead you into your assignment?
- ► Your whole life is a ministry; will you minister wherever you are?
- ► Would you connect with others and bring the kingdom to your locality?

∞

Activation

The Kingdom of God is filled with many vessels, each uniquely designed for different purposes. God has a vessel specifically for you, so sit with Him, ask Him what vessel He has created you to be, and make a list of all the qualities and gifts that comes to mind. Then, ask Him how your vessel can be used in the kingdom and which area he wants you to connect with.

∞∞∞

You saw who you created me to be before I became me! Before I'd ever seen the light of day, the number of days you planned for me were already recorded in your book.
Psalm 139:16, TPT

A Practical Guide
for Awareness
of the Abiding
Presence of God
in Your Everyday

Bible Study

Scriptures are God's profound way of engaging with us. These are His breathed (inspired) words breathed unto human authors to accomplish His purpose (2 Timothy 3:16). So, any Bible study time should primarily be focused on encountering the author of the Bible: God the Father, the Son and the Holy Spirit. Bible study goes beyond simply reading the Bible. Studying the Bible enables us to read and hear God's Word as the original recipients would have.

- **Practical items needed**: Have a Bible, preferably a paper copy in your preferred translation, along with a notebook, pen, highlighter, and a good study Bible for further reading if desired.

- **Invite God to speak:** Before you open your Bible, ask God to speak to you as you read. Keep a journal handy to note down any insights or messages that stand out. Always begin and end with God speaking to you through His Word.

- **Take your time:** Avoid rushing through scriptures or treat it as a mere checkbox task. Instead, focus on meeting God and seeking understanding from Him. While certain books, especially in the Old Testament, may seem challenging, remember that all the books are from God and have a purpose. Allow Him to bring understanding to you in His time.

- **Meditate on specific verses (exegesis):** Sometimes, it may be beneficial to focus on a particular verse and spend a significant amount of time meditating on it. Repeat the verse and compare it with other translations to gain deeper insights. Journal any new revelations or connections that come to light, as God will always reveal something unique to you.

- **Start from the New Testament and the Psalms:** If you're new to Bible study, beginning with the New Testament and the Psalms can provide a good foundation. You can also read these books alongside other books of the Bible and aim to dig deeper into the Word for better understanding. Books like John, Ephesians, and James are great to start with.

- **Focus on one book at a time:** My church has an initiative that encourages groups of three and four to get together and study a Bible book together. That has been so refreshing. Also, as part of our family devotion time, we read the Bible chronologically. We started from Genesis and went through a chapter or two daily, depending on how we all felt and learnt a lot. Challenging doing it with young ones, but it was rewarding. If this is new to you, I suggest doing that with others, as the discussions can be constructive.

- **Read the whole Bible:** If you are up for a challenge, you can embark on reading the entire Bible. While many plans are designed to be completed in a year, you can customize your plan to be more realistic, such as a Bible in two years plan. If you miss a day, simply reset and continue from where you left off.

- **Study with others for accountability and motivation:** In addition to your personal Bible study time, it may help to have someone alongside you doing the study together, especially if you want to focus on a specific book in the Bible or a specific topic. YouVersion offers various plans that you can invite others to join and study together.

DEEPER BIBLE STUDY

Several materials are available to delve deeper into the scriptures:

- **Bible Study Methods**: Explore various Bible study methods such as word study, topical study, character study, biographical study, verse-by-verse study, and more. Find one that suits you and dive into scriptures with it.

- **Concordance**: An exhaustive concordance, indexed to Strong's numbering system and containing Greek and Hebrew dictionaries, can provide valuable insights. This resource arranges Bible words in alphabetical order, giving you the original meaning and intention of the scriptures.

- **Bible Apps:** There are other useful apps and programs such as Blue Letter Bible (BLB), Logos, Mantis, and many others.

- **Lexicons**: Bible lexicons aid in comprehending the roots and fundamental meaning of the ancient language. They define and provide meaning to words from the Bible's original New Testament Greek and Old Testament Hebrew translations. Additionally, lexicons offer cultural context and insights that the authors wanted to convey.

- **Different translations**: Comparing any Bible passage with other translations is very rewarding. This approach often leads to profound revelations and a better understanding of the scriptures. There are three primary Bible translation styles which are:

  o **Word-for-word or literal translation:** These translations adhere closely to the original language, providing the most accurate representation of the original manuscripts. The text will be more challenging to read as it places importance on the original grammar and not English grammar. Examples are NASB, AMP, KJV, and others.

o **Thought-for-thought or dynamic equivalence**: These translations express the meaning of words or phrases from the original language in a comparable English manner. They are simpler to read as they do not strictly follow the original word grammar. Examples include NRSV, NIV, NLT, and others.

o **Paraphrase**: These translations amplify or expand on the words of the authors, aiming to aid readability and understanding. However, it is advisable to use paraphrases in conjunction with other translations to gain a deeper understanding. Examples are GNT, MSG, TPT, and others.

When studying the scriptures, you will find that there is never a dull moment. Follow the guidance of the Holy Spirit and do what works best for you.

Hearing from God

God is constantly speaking to us and it is essential for us to tune in and listen to what He has to say. He expresses Himself through all our senses (see, hear, feel & know). God reveals his secrets to His friends. His voice aligns with His character and is in agreement with His Word. Hearing Him speak deepens our understanding of who He is.

SEEING: God can reveal Himself to us through the wonders of nature, the prompting of the Holy Spirit, dreams, and visions (Joel 2:28-29, Jeremiah 1:11, Romans 1:20, Exodus 3:3, Habakkuk 2:1).

- **Dreams**: In the depths of the night, our Spirit actively interacts with God's Spirit. Whether you remember your dreams or not, it is important to recognize that God speaks through them. Keep a notebook or recording device nearby when you sleep, so you can capture what God reveals to you in the midst of your dreams. Many profound revelations have been released through my dreams. Even the title of this book was given to me in my sleep. You will be surprised by what you will hear.

- **Nature**: Take time to step outside and immerse yourself in the beauty of the natural world. Find a place of stillness, away from the hustle and bustle of the city, where you can breathe in the fresh air and connect with God. Whether it is an early morning walk as the sun rises or a peaceful evening stroll under the stars, God often reveals Himself through the intricate details of nature. Pay attention to the trees and the birds as they carry messages from Him.

- Sometimes, **an image** you hadn't thought of will come to mind. He loves to convey His messages through pictures and visions, providing glimpses of His plans and purposes.

HEARING: God's message may come to us audibly, as an inner prompting within our hearts, or even through the thoughts and impressions we receive. Additionally, God can use external sources such as people, songs, or movies to convey His truth and wisdom to us (John 10:27, Zephaniah 3:17).

- **Silence**: Creating moments of silence in our lives allows us to create space for God's voice to be heard. In the midst of chaos, it becomes impractical to hear anything He is saying. Take intentional time to steal away and listen to what He has to say.

- **Thoughts**: Whenever you find yourself alone, make space in your mind and let Him speak to you. Pay attention to the thoughts that arise within you and ask Him to help you discern which thoughts are from Him.

- **Words or phrases:** Sometimes, God highlights certain words or phrases in our surroundings. It could be a scripture or a specific word that catches your attention. He desires for you to explore and reflect on these words, inviting you into a deeper understanding of His message.

- **Praise and worship**: The lyrics of songs often carry profound messages about our situations. Surrounding yourself with praise and worship can create an atmosphere where God's voice can be heard. Recognize that God inspires artists to craft these words, making them a valuable source for gleaning His truth. It is important to note that God can even speak through secular songs, and I have personally experienced this countless times. Be open in whatever environment and make room to hear from Him.

- **Soak in spirit-driven podcasts or read spirit-inspired books**: God often uses people who have spent time with Him to speak to us, so embrace listening to podcasts or sermons from YouTube or reading books from trusted sources that are inspired by the Holy Spirit. These resources can provide valuable insights and guidance for those who seek a deep connection with God.

FEELING: There are times when we become acutely aware of other people's feelings and burdens. You may also feel a heightened awareness of God's presence. This can manifest as a stirring in your spirit, a deep sense of peace, or even goosebumps (2 Corinthians 2:14-15).

- **Sensations**: Sometimes, we can experience a deep sense of compassion or discern the atmosphere in a room. Pay attention to the sensations you feel in your body, as the Holy Spirit can move and communicate through your physical senses.

KNOWING /PERCEIVING: There are times when we simply know things, have premonitions, or receive words of knowledge. (Luke 11:17)

- **Knowledge and intuition**: Often, you may have a strong understanding or knowledge about something that you couldn't have come up with on your own. Frequently when something is missing at home, my daughter Kayla cheekily says, *"Mum, where is it?"*. This is because she recognizes that God often gives me insight into the location of misplaced items. This kind of knowledge is not limited to me, but it is a common way for God to interact with His children, especially women. If you have experienced this, recognize it as God's way of speaking and connecting with you.

Prayer time

In any relationship, the parties have to find a way to meaningfully express themselves to each other so they can have the most out of it. When it comes to our relationship with God, prayer serves as a vital form of conversation. Just as we would express ourselves to any other person, we can openly and honestly communicate with God, having faith that He hears and will respond to us (Matthew 7:7, Mark 11:22-2).

While there is no set standard for how we should communicate with God, it is vital to find ways that personally resonate with us. Each person may have a unique approach to prayer, and that is perfectly acceptable. It is about finding a method that allows for genuine expression and connection with God.

Personally, I have found certain ways of communicating with God to be particularly helpful, but they are not intended as standards for everyone.

- **Prayers can be quiet or loud**: Personally, I tend to have silent prayers when I am out and about, allowing my spirit to commune with God's Spirit. However, there are times when I feel compelled to express my prayers loudly, depending on my surroundings. Right in my home is the most comfortable place, and so I find it easy to burst out in prayer.

- **Prayer turns all thoughts to God**: Turn all your thoughts to prayer, especially any worries. Instead of thinking through something unpleasant, talk to him about it. Express any feelings and fears to God. Even when contemplating my daily plans and tasks, I make it a habit to involve God in the process, seeking His guidance and wisdom (1 Thessalonians 5:17).

- **Prayer mostly begins with thanking Him**: Every good thing is from above, so for everything you experience, thank God. Let thanksgiving override all the words you say to God. Whether it's someone's kind gesture or the love shown by my children, express your gratitude to God for His hand in these moments (Psalm 68:19).

- **Prayer involves worship and praise**: Worshipping and praising God helps ease us into what we want to pray about. It is essential to exalt God above everything else in your life. By placing God in the highest place in your life, you will be rightly positioned to see Him right. If you struggle with this, turn to the Psalms as a source of inspiration and return these words of praise and adoration to God (Psalm 69:30-31, Hebrews 13:15).

- **Prayer involves speaking in tongues**: If you have the gift of praying in the Spirit, embrace the freedom to pray in this way wherever and whenever you feel led. Your tongues is a spiritual language only heaven understands and will be the best form of prayer. I personally prioritize allowing my tongues to guide my prayer sessions, as it connects my spirit with God's (1 Corinthians 14:2, 13-15).

- **Prayer mainly involves praying for others**: Sometimes God will impress a longing in your heart to pray for something or somebody. This is known as intercession. Make time and pray about it. Remember that it is not about your words but your heart posture interacting with the Spirit of God. Let the Spirit guide you to pray as He wills; starting with tongues if necessary (1 Timothy 2:1).

- **Prayers have no room for doubt**: Refuse to doubt anything you have prayed about. When you start feeling doubtful, ask God to help you. He might cause you to remember other ways He has come through for you to encourage you. But whatever that looks like, do not doubt that God is listening, and He will come through for you (1 John 5:14-15, 2 Corinthians 10:3-5).

Fasting

Biblical fasting is more than simply going without food or dieting, it involves refraining from food for a spiritual reason.

- **Fasting was first mentioned by Jesus** in his Sermon on the Mount, where He discussed prayer, almsgiving, and fasting. Jesus implied that we are required to fast as God's children to strengthen our relationship with God, to pray and connect with a Father, and to give to good works. We should fast as a part of a normal Christian lifestyle because it allows us to build an intimate relationship with God the Father and experience God in a more profound way than we might otherwise. In either case, fasting can be a personal, intimate act or a communal act, in which several people give up food together.

- **God wants you to fast because of the blessings** that will flow into your life as a result. Fasting does not require a profound spiritual epiphany. You should fast if you desire to draw closer to your heavenly Father. Moreover, God undeniably guarantees that you will receive heavenly blessings when you fast properly and with the appropriate intentions. *"God is a rewarder."* Therefore, the Father will reward you if you seek him (Hebrews 12:1).

- **We must take care of our bodies** since they are the temples of the Holy Spirit, and fasting allows us to keep our bodies healthy and free of toxins so that they can function properly. You also give your body the chance to recover and regenerate the way you want it to. The less food you consume, the more space God has to cleanse your spirit of any foreign impurities. In addition to detoxifying your body, fasting improves your mental acuity and heals your body physically.

- **Fasting also keeps our hearts humble**. It brings us closer to God as it helps in our knowledge and understanding of what the Father is expressing to us. Through this experience, you engage with the scriptures and thereby learn more about the Father. You discover God's will for your life by submitting your will during a fasting period. Fasting prepares the way for God to give you a fresh revelation, a fresh vision, and a clear purpose. Jesus experienced this after his 40-day fast in the wilderness (Luke 4).

- **By fasting, you sacrifice yourself,** think about others, and have time to reflect on what God wants for the world around you. As a result, you can pray and act as an intermediary for others. He also indicated that some supernatural breakthroughs can only be achieved when we fast and pray (Matthew 17:15). There are financial blessings that are released when we fast. Plant the seed of faith and be expectant of the goodness of the Lord during the fast.

101 of Fasting

- **Plan the fast**: You want to have an aim for the fast, and it is vital to plan for it, especially so you know if it has been successful. Planning will also help you have all the required materials needed for the fast (Habakkuk 2:2).

- **Types of fast**: There are three main types of fast. These are absolute (no food or water), normal (no food but water) and partial (limited food and water). Your choice of fast should be guided by the Holy Spirit, as each requires a sacrifice. Seek guidance from God in determining the appropriate type of fast for you.

- **Length of fast - Half day/full day**: You choose your fast according to your ability and what you feel led to do. God is interested in your choice of fast, so let Him guide you. Don't go for an extended period if that is not your thing.

- **Commit to spending time alone with God**: A meaningful fast should set a time to meet with God. You will need to say no to phones, social media, or any distractions during that period. If you want to hear what God has to say, you must create that moment.

- **Practical elements**: Have a notebook, pens and pencils, and journal your thoughts, experiences, prayers and what God does and speaks to you.

- **Spend time in the Word:** God mostly speaks through His Word, so spend some time in the scriptures. Have some scriptures ready, meditate on them and pray with the Word.

- **Fluid day**: Stay hydrated throughout the fast by consuming plenty of fluids. Expect some discomfort, such as headaches and hunger pangs, but remember that these sensations can subside as you continue to pray. Understand that these discomforts are often your body's way of detoxifying.

- **Commit to praying for others:** Praying for others is more rewarding than focussing on yourself, especially those you want to see saved. Of course, pray for yourself but let that not be all you do during fasting. Let the Spirit lead you on what to pray about.

- **Pray more or less**: Let your spirit flow with the Spirit of God. Sometimes you will be prompted to deep prayers, while at other times, you may find it difficult to pray at all. Be gentle with yourself, as God is more concerned with your heart posture and sacrifice than a particular prayer format.

- **Answered prayers**: If you don't see immediate answers to your prayers during the fasting period, do not be discouraged. Remember that you may be sowing seeds that God will water and bring to fruition in His timing, which may be different from your own. Trust that God hears and will answer your prayers in His perfect way and timing.

Here are some scriptures to aid a fast

Romans 8:28-31, Isaiah 55:8-13, Jeremiah 6:16, Is 61:1-4, Isaiah 11:2, Psalm 51:10-12, Ezekiel 36:26-28, Romans 12:1-2, Colossians 3:1-3, Ephesians 6:10-17, John 10:14-18, 1 John 4:7-21, Psalms 42:1-2, Matthew 5:6, Matthew 17:20-21.

Wealth Mindset

A wealthy mindset sees an unlimited God with unlimited resources who desires to generously provide for you. Through Christ Jesus, my God will fulfil all your needs according to His glorious riches. (Philippians 4:19)

- **God is good**: He is a constant source of goodness and desires to fill your life with abundance. By living in His goodness, you can fulfil the purpose He created you for and be a blessing to others. Every good and perfect gift comes from above, from the Father of lights (James 1:17).

- **God is the owner**: To experience the blessings of financial abundance fully, it is essential to acknowledge God as your ultimate source. Everything in your possession belongs to Him and is intended for His use. Your role is to act as a responsible steward and ensure He remains the sole owner of all your possessions. Invite the Spirit to lead and guide you in managing your finances. Make God the centre of every financial decision. True financial freedom comes from seeking God's kingdom first (Matthew 6:33).

- **God wants you to prosper**: Prosperity is having more than enough to serve in the assignment God has given you. Prosperity starts from believing who you are in Christ and not what you have in your possession. God wants you to live in abundant wealth through Him. You do not need to be poor for God to bless you, and He does not want your focus solely on accumulating wealth (the spirit of mammon). Instead, you need to seek Him out and live in His presence to live a rich and fulfilling life. Just as parents want their children to have all their heart's desires, God also desires for you to live a life of abundance. The key to achieving this is by seeking Him first and prioritising Him in everything you do.

- **Your financial blessings are meant to serve a greater purpose:** It is important to remember that everything you have is a blessing from God, and it is your responsibility to use it to bless others. Therefore, when making financial plans, it is vital to think beyond your own needs and consider how you can help others. Your role is to be a conduit of blessings, not a storage tank. When prompted by the Holy Spirit, freely pour out what God has entrusted to you.

- **Giving should be guided by the Holy Spirit:** It is not necessary for you to support every ministry but listen to God's leading on where to invest your resources. Always remember that God knows the exact needs and the best way to meet them. You will continue to offer support for any issues or situations that arise. However, you will take on the role of a steward and address specific problems brought to your attention. You will not feel guilty for being unable to assist someone. As members of God's kingdom, we all have a specific role to play. If you allow God to guide your desires, He will lead you towards experiences that bear fruit, as He knows what is best for you.

  o Therefore, wherever God has appointed you and planted you, that is where you will sow into to see a bountiful harvest. It is best to start by sowing into your local church, where you receive spiritual nourishment and support. This is a great way to give back and help sustain the community that supports you. If you are attending a church that is not providing you with spiritual nourishment and feel depleted, it may be time to return to the beginning and seek guidance from God about finding the proper environment to grow in.

  o Outside the church, any institution or initiative the

Holy Spirit prompts you to support will be the next thing to focus on. Essentially, the fruits of sowing can only be yielded if we are connected to the right soil.

o   Additionally, there will always be various needs in your surroundings. Therefore, allocating a percentage of your resources, guided by the Holy Spirit, is important to attend to these needs. This can apply to your family, friends, or institutions that serve these needs. Ultimately, allow your spirit to lead you in your actions. It is important to note that some individuals choose to disregard God's laws and refuse to work. Remember the saying, "No work, no eat," Be cautious about investing your finances in such areas, as it may not yield positive results.

- **The amount you give is not as important as the heart behind your giving:** Do not let the amount you wish to sow dictate your giving; instead, examine the underlying reasons behind your generosity. We choose to give because it comes from the goodness of our hearts, and God has instilled this desire within us. The amount we give is entirely up to us, as it should bring us happiness and deepen our faith. No one else can determine the amount we give (2 Corinthians 9:6).

- **Tithing:** God loves you regardless of whether you give or not. Expressing our love to Him through giving is one way He channels abundance into our lives. Give according to your ability. Let your generosity reflect your devotion. Whilst it is recommended to sow at least 10% of your income, it is necessary to let the Holy Spirit guide you in determining the exact percentage that should go towards your designated field. Investing that 10% into the place where you are receiving spiritual nourishment is crucial. When you realise that God is the source of your wealth, giving back 10% of your money to Him will not be a burden, as you do it out of your love and gratitude for Him (2 Corinthians 8:3).

- **Never give under pressure:** It is essential to discern when you feel prompted by the Spirit to give versus when you may be feeling manipulated. It is never a good idea to give to anyone or any organisation under compulsion, as there is no real blessing in doing so. You have to offer from a generous heart. Remember, the money comes from God and you do not need to feel pressured or manipulated to give it back to Him. His Spirit will guide you and show you when and where it is appropriate to give. Do not give with the sole motivation and purpose of receiving blessings from God. Instead, remember that God wants to bless you with His resources (2 Corinthians 9:7).

- **Cultivate a giving grace:** If you regularly give, embark on a spiritual journey with God to enhance your ability to give gracefully. Develop a generous heart and be open to giving without hesitation or discomfort. When you give gracefully, you offer your gifts freely without expecting anything in return. Your motive for giving is simply because you love your Heavenly Father (2 Corinthians 8:7) .

- **Understand the principle of sowing and reaping:** When you plant a seed, you can expect a bountiful harvest with proper care. Farmers do not simply plant a seed and leave it; they nurture it until it blossoms into a fruitful harvest. Similarly, when you sow your resources in fertile soil, you can be sure to reap a plentiful harvest. It is impossible for you to surpass God in giving, so you can anticipate He will bless you when you give (Luke 6:38).

- **Plan to wisely invest your money:** Remember to allocate your resources towards sowing, saving, and spending wisely. Be faithful with the resources you have and seek wise financial stewardship.

- **Release fear of money**: Let go of your fear or anxiety you may have about money and instead place your trust in God, who knows all things and has the power to resolve any issues. Trusting in God will help you overcome any limitations that may be holding you back (Matthew 6:25).

- **Embrace the dry seasons as preparation**: During dry seasons, it's important not to dwell on lack, but rather see it as preparation for a bountiful harvest. Be prepared with the necessary tools and remain faithful during challenging times, knowing that God's timing is perfect.

Biblical Truths

- 2 Corinthians 8 & 9

- Proverbs 3:9-10, 16, Proverbs 6:6, 10-11, Proverbs 8:18, 20-21, Proverbs 10:4, 6, 21-22, Proverbs 11: 25, 28, Proverbs 13:11, 22, Proverbs 15:6, Proverbs 16:8, Proverbs 18:11, Proverbs 19:11, Proverbs 22:1,4.

- Abraham – Genesis 13, Isaac – Genesis 26:12-13, Joseph – Genesis 39:2, Obed-Edom – 2 Samuel 6:11, Solomon – 2 Chronicles 1:10-12

ADDITIONAL COPYRIGHTS

- Amplified Bible, Classic Edition (AMPC) - Copyright © 1954, 1958, 1962, 1964, 1965, 1987 by The Lockman Foundation.
- Easy-to-Read Version (ERV) - Copyright © 2006 by Bible League International.
- English Standard Version (ESV) - The Holy Bible, English Standard Version. ESV® Text Edition: 2016. Copyright © 2001 by Crossway Bibles, a publishing ministry of Good News Publishers.
- GOD'S WORD Translation (GW) - Copyright © 1995, 2003, 2013, 2014, 2019, 2020 by God's Word to the Nations Mission Society. All rights reserved.
- Good News Translation (GNT) - Good News Translation® (Today's English Version, Second Edition) © 1992 American Bible Society. All rights reserved.
- International Children's Bible (ICB) - The Holy Bible, International Children's Bible® Copyright© 1986, 1988, 1999, 2015 by Thomas Nelson. Used by permission.
- International Standard Version (ISV) - Copyright © 1995-2014 by ISV Foundation. ALL RIGHTS RESERVED INTERNATIONALLY. Used by permission of Davidson Press, LLC.

ABOUT THE AUTHOR

Hello, I am Cathy, chosen by God to devote my heart solely to Him. I firmly believe that seeking intimacy with God is the path to true fulfilment. I delight in sharing positivity with those around me. It is my passion to help others break free from sin and experience breakthroughs in their lives. My ultimate prayer is for all of God's children to encounter His boundless grace, love, joy, and peace.

I am part of GCSSM, an online school that has shaped my identity and ignited a passion for animation and writing.

I am married to the wonderful Ebenezer Nortey, and we are honoured to use our spiritual gifts to positively impact others. Our amazing children are witnesses to the incredible ways that God works in our lives.

I am a Health Physicist who enjoys inspiring young people in STEM.

We would love for you to stay connected with us, so please visit our website at https://www.sevenflamingtorches.com to sign up for our mailing list and be the VIP of our community with exclusive access to our uplifting blog posts and valuable resources that will help you strengthen your intimacy with God. But wait, there's more! Tune in to our YouTube channel for uplifting videos as well as animated Bible stories.

Thank you for your support and blessings to you.

Printed in Great Britain
by Amazon

30168954R00086